ARIZONA RENTAL RIGHTS

A Guide Book for Tenants, Landlords and Mobile Home Users

David A. Peterson
Andrew M. Hull

ARIZONA RENTAL RIGHTS

Copyright © 2000 by David Peterson and Andrew Hull

Revised Editions
1988, 1990, 1993

TO ORDER ADDITIONAL COPIES CALL: 1-800-521-9221 OR ASK FOR THE BOOK AT ANY BOOKSTORE.

ISBN 1-55838-191-0

Published in the United States of America

Table of Contents

Table of Contents iii
Disclosure vi
Acknowledgments vii
Preface vii
Moving In 1
   Landlord Identification and Disclosure 1
Rental Agreement 3
   Terms and Conditions 3
Rules and Regulations 4
Tenant's Legal Obligations 5
Landlord's Legal Obligations 6
   Security Deposits 7
   Landlord to Supply Possession of Dwelling Unit 8
   Landlord to Maintain Fit Premises 9
   Limitation of Liability 10
   Prohibited Provisions 10
Abandonment 11
   Waiver of Landlord's Right to Terminate 13
   Landlord Liens 14
   Remedy after Termination 14
   Recovery of Possession Limited 14
   Access 14
Landlord's Rights 16
   Noncompliance with Rental Agreement by Tenant 16
   Failure to Maintain 19
Tenant's Rights 20
   Noncompliance by the Landlord 20
   Failure to Deliver Possession 22
   Self-Help for Minor Defects 22
   Utility Problems 23
   Landlord's Noncompliance —
      Defense to Action for Possession 24
   Fire or Casualty Damage 25
   Remedies for Landlord's Unlawful Ouster 25
Discrimination and Minors 26
Notice 27
Retaliatory Action 29

Top 10 — Do's and Don't's 30
Rental Increase 32
Moving Out 32
    Periodic Tenancy... 32
Forcible Entry and Detainer (Eviction)..................... 34
    Acts Which Constitute 34
    Definition of Forcible Entry 34
    Definition of Forcible Detainer 35
    Additional Definitions.................................... 35
    Complaint and Answer.................................... 36
Special Detainer Action 37
Going to Court 39
    Trial Procedure 39
    Postponement 39
    Judgment 40
    Appeal 40
    Stay of Proceedings 42
    Trial and Judgment of Appeal......................... 42
    Appeal to Supreme Court 42
    Other Proceedings.. 43
Top 10 — Going to Court 44
General Provisions... 45
Humorous Examples 47
Mobile Home Parks 55
    Introduction.. 55
Mobile Home Rental Agreement 56
    Terms and Conditions 56
    Utility Charges 58
    Guest Fees 58
    Prohibited Provisions 58
    Separation of Rents 59
    Regulation of Rents....................................... 59
Landlord's Obligations 60
    Security Deposits... 60
    Disclosure of Rental Agreement 60
    Possession of Mobile Home Space 62
    Maintain Fit Premises 62
    Limitation of Liability 63
    Statement of Policy 63

Educational Requirements for Park Managers 64
Tenant's Obligation 64
    Tenant to Maintain Space 64
    Rules and Regulations 65
    Access 67
    Tenant Use 67
Landlord's Rights and Remedies 68
    Termination or Nonrenewal of Lease Agreement 68
Tenant's Rights and Remedies 70
    Noncompliance by Landlord 70
    Wrongful Failure to Supply Service 71
    Tenant's Remedies 71
    Change in Use 72
    Mobile Home Relocation Fund 74
    Assessments for Fund 75
    Failure to Maintain 78
    Remedies for Abandonment 78
    Recovery of Possession Limited 79
    Periodic Tenancy 79
    Remedies for Abuse of Access 80
Retaliatory Action 81
Mobile Home Parks Hearing Officer Function 82
    Establishment and Duties 82
    Rights and Procedures 82
    Orders, Penalties, Disposition 83
    Scope of Hearing 83
    Rehearing 84
Top 10 Tips for Landlords and Tenants of Mobile Homes 85
Commercial Leases 86
Bankruptcy 86
General Provisions 87
General Definitions Part 1 89
General Definitions Part 2 91
Slumlord Laws 94
Sample Forms 96
Informational Agencies and Numbers 112

DISCLOSURE

The Arizona State legislature may enact changes to the laws as currently covered in this book. The authors have no control over these changes. This book will be updated from time to time as is necessary. Also, the opinions of the authors may not to apply each personís specific situation. Therefore, it is always advised that you consult an attorney for more specific advice.

I dedicate this edition to the memory of my father Robert Earl Peterson, Sr. who made growing-up wonderful while showing me love and support with every adventure I took.

David A. Peterson

I dedicate this book to my family, especially my wife, Vickie, without whom life would be meaningless, my children, Bryce, Bodie, Bonnie and Brooke, to my parents Joe and Nancy, my brothers MacKay, Willard and Jonathan, and to the Good Lord who has blessed me with the most wonderful family anyone could ever deserve.

Andrew M. Hull

Preface

Individuals who rent or people who rent to others have some basic legal rights. If a problem does arise, talk it out first. If you cannot resolve the disagreement among yourselves, then know the proper procedure to follow so you can protect your rights and at the same time proceed more efficiently. This book is intended for the benefit of all tenants, students, and mobile home users, as well as the landlords and managers of these individuals.

Throughout this book, reference will be made to the Ariona Residential Landlord and Tenant Act and also to Mobile Home Parks Residential Landlord and Tenant Acts. They can be identified by statute numbers and will be referred to as sections or chapters. (Arizona Revised Statutes referred to as A.R.S.)

Residential Landlord Tenant Section

Residential Landlord Tenant Act
(Generally houses or apartments)

Moving In

Before moving in, there are a few things you should remember to do.

1. Visit and walk through the actual unit you will be living in, not another one just like it. Make a list of needed repairs and have the landlord or manager sign it so that you cannot be charged later for the damage. The landlord must provide a move in/move out statement to the tenant at the inception of the lease. Talk with prospective neighbors about the living conditions and criticisms they might have.

2. If you agree to improvements or repairs on the rental unit, such as painting, make sure the details are in writing and signed by the landlord. All improvements must be approved ahead of time by the landlord, especially if you want to be reimbursed for materials and/or labor. Keep receipts and records of the time and money spent to support your efforts.

3. If the rental unit is unusually dirty when you move in, notify the landlord at once. It is their duty to see that it is cleaned, or compensate you through a rent adjustment for doing the work. If they refuse, you should keep a record of the time and money you spend, as well as taking photographs, have witnesses view your rental unit, in case court action is every instigated by the landlord or yourself.

4. Landlord identification and disclosure is required by law *(A.R.S. Section 33-1322).*

   a. The landlord or any person authorized to enter into a rental agreement on his behalf shall disclose to the tenant in writing at or before the commencement of the tenancy the name and address of each of the following:
   (1) The person authorized to manage the premises.
   (2) An owner of the premises or a person authorized by to act on behalf of the owner for the purpose of being served

1

with lawsuits and for the purpose of receiving and receipting for notices and demands.

b. Any owner or agent is required to keep current this information and furnish to the tenant upon request.

c. A person who fails to comply with the above becomes an agent of each person who is landlord for the following purposes:

(1) Service of process of lawsuits and receiving and receipting for notices and demands.

(2) Performing the obligations of the landlord under rental agreement and expending or making available for the purpose all rent collected from the premises.

d. If there is a written rental agreement, the landlord must tender and deliver a signed copy of the rental agreement to the tenant and the tenant must sign and deliver to the landlord one fully executed copy of such rental agreement within a reasonable time after the agreement is executed. A written rental agreement shall have all blank spaces completed. Noncompliance with this subsection shall be deemed a material noncompliance by the landlord or the tenant, as the case may be, of the rental agreement. If there is a material noncompliance, then either party must give the noncomplying party proper notification under A.R.S. Section 33-1361 or 33-1368 of the Landlord tenant Act (which provisions are set forth under later sections dealing with landlord and tenant noncompliance).

5. Determine in advance that you are able to make the rent payments.

6. Read the agreement carefully.

7. Keep a copy of everything.

8. Look for an automatic renewal clause. Some leases state that the lease will renew itself for the same length of time if the tenant does not notify the landlord otherwise. Ready your lease to see what steps are necessary to either renew it or terminate it.

9. See if there are any provisions for breaking the lease. Usually there are not and either party must follow the procedures as set forth in the Landlord and Tenant Act.

10. Ask about policies, rules and regulations regarding the towing of vehicles. *(See humorous example pg. 47)*

The Rental Agreement

Terms and Conditions of Rental Agreement

a. The tenant and a landlord may include in a rental agreement any terms and conditions not prohibited by the Landlord and Tenant Act or other rules of law including rent, term of the agreement, and other provisions governing the rights and obligations of the parties.

b. In absence of a rental agreement, the tenant shall pay as rent the fair rental value for the use and occupancy of the dwelling unit.

c. Rent shall be payable without demand or notice at the time and place agreed upon by the parties. Unless otherwise agreed, rent is payable to the manager or owner at their dwelling unit and periodic rent is payable at the beginning of any term of one month or less and otherwise is equally monthly installments at the beginning of each month. Unless otherwise agreed, rent shall be uniformly apportionable from day to day.

d. Unless the rental agreement fixes a definite term (i.e., 6 months), the tenancy shall be week to week in case of a roomer who pays weekly rent, and in all other cases month to month. *(See A.R.S. Section 33-1314)*

e. Where either the landlord or his agent makes oral representation with regard to any terms of the lease, those oral representations become part of the lease even though they are not written into the lease. However, it is best to reduce these to writing or confirm by letter.

f. The purpose of any nonrefundable security deposit must now be stated in writing.

g. The tenant must be told in writing they can get a free copy of the Arizona Residential Landlord and Tenant Act free from the Arizona Secretary of State's Office.

h. The lease must state any change in rent; sales tax can be passed on to the tenant (with 30 days written notice).

However, it is always a good idea to have any oral representations reduced to writing and written in the rental agreement. Keep in mind that if the landlord uses or incorporates in the written rental agreement any provision prohibited by the Landlord and Tenant Act, that the provision becomes unenforceable and the tenant may have a claim against the landlord for 2 months' rent for using an illegal provision.

(See humorous example pg. 47)

IT'S ALL QUITE SIMPLE...
Rules and Regulations

a. A landlord from time to time, with 30 days written notice, may adopt rules and regulations, however described, concerning the tenant's use and occupancy of the premises. Such rules or regulations are enforceable against the tenant only if:

1. Their purpose is to promote the convenience, safety or welfare of the tenants in the premises, preserve the landlord's property from abusive use or make a fair distribution of services and facilities held out for the tenants generally.
2. They are reasonably related to the purpose for which adopted.
3. They apply to all tenants in the premises in a fair manner.

4. They are sufficiently explicit in prohibition, direction, or limitation of the tenant's conduct to fairly inform him of what he must or must not do to comply.
5. They are not for the purpose of evading the legal obligation for the landlord.
6. The tenant has notice of them at the time he enters into the rental agreement.

b.   A rule or regulation adopted after the tenant enters into the rental agreement is enforceable against the tenant if reasonable notice of its adoption is given to the tenant and it does not work a substantial modification of his rental agreement. Normally, if the landlord wishes to change existing rules or regulations or add to those currently in existence, he must give the tenant at least thirty (30) days prior written notice to the date the rules and regulations will become effective. It is also advisable that all rules and regulations always be reduced to writing and copies provided to all tenants. *(See A.R.S. Section 33-1342)* Keep in mind a landlord cannot use rules and regulations to change a material term of the lease (i.e. amount of late charges, rental due date, etc.).

(See humorous example pg. 48)

Tenant's Legal Obligations

The Landlord and Tenant Act requires that the tenant shall maintain their dwelling unit as follows:

1. Comply with all obligations primarily imposed upon tenants by applicable provisions of building codes materially affecting health and safety.

2. Keep that part of the premises that he occupies and uses as clean and safe as the conditions of the premises permit.

3. Dispose from his dwelling unit all ashes, rubbish, garbage and other waste in a clean and safe manner.

4. Keep all plumbing fixtures in the dwelling unit or used by the tenant as clean as their condition permits.

5. Use in a reasonable manner all electrical, plumbing, sanitary, heating, ventilating, air conditioning, and other facilities and appliance including elevators in the premises.

6. Not deliberately or negligently destroy, deface, damaged, impair or remove any part of the premises or knowingly permit any person to do so.

7. Conduct himself and require other persons on the premises with his consent to conduct themselves in a manner that will not disturb his neighbor's peaceful enjoyment of the premises. *(See A.R.S. Section 33-1341)*

Also, a tenant is now held responsible for the conduct of their guests if the tenant knew or should have known the guest would engage in certain prohibited conduct, or the tenant took no steps to stop their guest. *(See A.R.S. Section 33-1368G)*

It is this section of law that the landlord may make deductions out of a tenant's security deposit for any damages incurred by the landlord. Therefore it is important that the tenant understand what their legal obligations are. Also, it is this section that the landlord most often gives tenants noncompliance types of notices to terminate the tenant's rental obligations. For instance, a tenant who constantly plays his stereo loud or has guests coming and going at all hours of the night, could be cited under Paragraph 7 above.

THAT SHOULD COVER YOUR DEPOSIT!

Landlord's Legal Obligations

Security Deposits *(A.R.S. Section 33-1321)*

a. A landlord shall not demand or receive security, however denominated, including but not limited to prepaid rent in an amount or value in excess of one and one-half month's rent. A tenant may voluntarily pay more than one and one-half month's rent in advance, and if accepted by the Landlord, the Landlord is not in violation of this section. A security deposit normally is cash, but does not have to be. The landlord can accept anything of value, i.e., stereo, television.

b. Cleaning and redecorating deposit, if nonrefundable, must be so stated in writing by the landlord along with their purpose. Cleaning and redecorating deposits are not considered security and any amount can be collected so long as it is reasonable. Also, the landlord need not account for the deposit at he must do for security under Section C.

c. Upon termination of the tenancy, property or money held by the landlord as prepaid rent and security may be applied to the payment of any charges and damages which the landlord has suffered by reason of the tenant's noncompliance with Section 33-1341 or their rental agreement *(see Tenant's Legal Obligations)* all as itemized by the landlord in a written notice delivered to the tenant together with the amount of refund due within fourteen business days after termination of the tenancy and delivery of possession and demand by the tenant. Demand must be in writing and delivered personally or mailed by registered or certified mail *(See A.R.S. Section 33-1313(B).*

d. If the landlord fails to comply by either returning the security or delivering a written itemization, the tenant may recover the property and money due him together with damages in an amount equal to twice the amount wrongfully withheld.

e.   This section does not preclude the landlord or tenant from recovering other damages to which he may be entitled under the Landlord and Tenant Act.

f.   The holder of the landlord's interest in the premises at the time of the termination of the tenancy is bound by this section. What this means is that if the property is sold, the new owner is responsible to the tenant for the return of the deposit or any itemization of damages that is required. Also, only the actual owner of the property is liable, not a manager or property supervisor if the owner's name is disclosed at the beginning of the lease.

This paragraph of the Landlord and Tenant Act probably generates more litigation in Small Claims Court than any other. If you are a tenant, you must comply with three obligations. 1) Termination of your tenancy; 2) Return of possession to the landlord; and 3) Make a written demand for your deposit sent either Certified or Registered Mail or delivered in hand. If you are a landlord, you want to make sure that you can support any and all damages and that your damages are beyond normal wear and tear. Additionally, the tenant must show that you have "wrongfully" withheld the tenant's deposit. Finally, the awarding of double damages is discretionary with the Court, not mandatory. Simply because the landlord has been a few days late in returning a deposit does not mean the tenant will be awarded their deposit plus double that amount. In addition, a landlord may deduct out of a tenant's deposit the balance of a lease, if the tenant prematurely moves out. The landlord is under a duty to use reasonable efforts to re-rent the premises.

(See humorous example pg. 48)

Landlord to Supply Possession of Dwelling Unit
(A.R.S. Section 33-1323)

a.   At the beginning of the term of the tenancy, the landlord shall deliver possession of the premises to the tenant in compliance with the rental agreement and the landlord's duty to deliver the premises in a fit and habitable condition. The landlord may bring an action for possession against any person wrongfully in possession and may recover damages provided in Section 33-1375, subsection C *(see Moving Out).*

Landlord to Maintain Fit Premises
(A.R.S. Section 33-1324)

a. The landlord shall:
1. Maintain the premises so that they comply with the requirements of applicable building codes materially affecting health and safety.
2. Make all repairs and do whatever is necessary to put and keep the premises in a fit and habitable condition.
3. Keep all common areas of the premises in a clean and safe condition.
4. Maintain in good and safe working order and condition all electrical, plumbing, sanitary, heating, ventilating, air-conditioning, and other facilities and appliances, including elevators, supplied or required to be supplied by him.
5. Provide and maintain appropriate receptacles and conveniences for the removal of ashes, garbage, rubbish and other waste incidental to the occupancy of the dwelling unit and arrange for their removal.
6. Supply running water and reasonable amounts of hot water at all times, reasonable heat and reasonable air-conditioning or cooling where such units are installed and offered, when required by seasonal weather conditions.

b. The landlord and tenant of a single family residence (not applicable to apartments) may agree in writing, supported by adequate consideration, that the tenant perform the landlord's duties specified in subsection A, paragraphs 5 and 6 and also specified repairs, maintenance tasks, alterations and remodeling, but only if the transaction is entered into in good faith, not for the purpose of evading the obligations of the landlord and the work is not necessary to cure noncompliance with subsection A, paragraph 1 and 2 above. If such an agreement is entered into, reduce it to writing and make sure all parties sign the agreement.

c. The landlord and tenant of any dwelling unit other than a single family residence may agree that the tenant is to perform specified repairs, maintenance tasks, alterations or remodeling only if:
1. The agreement of the parties is entered into in good faith and not for the purpose of evading the obligations of the landlord, and is set forth in a separate writing signed by the parties and supported by adequate consideration.
2. The work is not necessary to cure noncompliance with

subsection A, paragraph 1 and 2.

3. The agreement does not diminish or affect the obligation of the landlord to other tenants in the premises.

The landlord should take all reasonable steps to make repairs and do whatever is necessary to keep the tenant's premises in a fit and habitable condition. If the tenant makes a demand for repairs, the landlord should make those repairs so long as the request is legitimate. It is advisable that the landlord document each an every repair request in the tenant's file so that the landlord is in a position to prove that they have adequately responded to repair requests.

Limitation of Liability *(A.R.S. Section 33-1325)*

a. Unless otherwise agreed, a landlord who conveys premises that include a dwelling unit subject to a rental agreement in good faith sale to a bona fide purchaser is relieved of liability under the rental agreement and this chapter as to events occurring subsequent to written notice to the tenant of the conveyance. He remains liable to the tenant for any property and money to which the tenant is entitled under A.R.S. Section 33-1321 *(see Security Deposits).*

Prohibited Provisions in Rental Agreement
(A.R.S. Section 33-1315)

a. A rental agreement shall not provide that the tenant does any of the following:

1. Agrees to waive or forego rights or remedies under the Landlord and Tenant Act.

2. Agrees to pay the landlord's attorney's fees, except an agreement in writing may provide that the attorney's fees may be awarded to the prevailing party in the event of court action, and except that a prevailing party in a contested forcible detainer is eligible to be awarded attorney's fees pursuant to Section 12-341.01 (A.R.S.) regardless of whether the rental agreement provides for such an award.

3. Agrees to the exculpation or limitation of any liability of the landlord arising under law or to indemnify the landlord for that liability or the costs connected therewith.

b. A provision prohibited by subsection A of this section included in a rental agreement is unenforceable. If a landlord deliberately uses a rental agreement containing provision known by him to be prohibited, the tenant may recover actual damages sustained by him and not more than two month's periodic rent.

Abandonment *(A.R.S. 33-1370)*

Sec. 6, Title 33, Chapter 10, Article 4, Arizona Revised Statutes Abandonment; *(A.R.S. Section 33-1370)*

a. If a dwelling unit is abandoned after the time prescribed in subsection H of this section, the landlord shall send the tenant a notice of abandonment by certified mail, return receipt requested, addressed to the tenant's last known address and to any of the tenant's alternate addresses known to the landlord. The landlord shall also post a notice of abandonment on the door to the dwelling unit or any other conspicuous place on the property for five days.

b. Five days after notice of abandonment has been both posted and mailed, the landlord may retake the dwelling unit and rerent the dwelling unit at a fair rental value if no personal property remains in the dwelling unit. After the landlord retakes the dwelling unit, money held by the landlord as a security deposit is forfeited and shal' be applied to the payment of any accrued rent and other reasonable cots incurred by the landlord by reason of the tenant's abandonment.

c. If the tenant abandons the dwelling unit, the landlord shall make reasonable efforts to rent it at a fair rental. If the landlord rents the dwelling unit for a term beginning prior to the expiration of the rental agreement, it is deemed to be terminated as of the date the new tenancy begins. If the landlord fails to use reasonable efforts to rent the dwelling unit at a fair rental or if the landlord accepts the abandonment as a surrender, the rental agreement is deemed to be terminated by the landlord as of the date the landlord has notice of the abandonment. If the tenancy if from month-to-month or week-to-week, the term of the rental agreement for this purpose shall be deemed to be a month or a week, as the case may be.

d. After the landlord has retaken possession of the dwelling unit, the landlord may remove all personal property left by the tenant in the dwelling unit. The landlord shall notify the tenant of the location of the personal property in the same manner prescribed in subsection A.

e.   The landlord shall hold the tenant's personal property for a period of twenty-one days beginning of the first rental due date occurring after the landlords' declaration of abandonment.   The landlord shall use reasonable care in holding the tenant's personal property. If the landlord holds the property for this twenty-one day period and the tenant makes no reasonable effort to recover it, the landlord may sell the property, retain the proceeds, and apply them towards the tenant's outstanding rent. If provided by a written rental agreement, the landlord may destroy or otherwise dispose of some or all of the property if the landlord reasonably determines that the value of the property is so low that the cost of moving, storage, and conducting a public sale exceeds the amount that would be realized from the sale.

f.   For a period of twelve months after the sale the landlord shall:

1. Keep adequate records of the outstanding and unpaid rent and the sale of the tenant's personal property.
2. Hold any excess proceeds for the benefit of the tenant.

g.   If the tenant notifies the landlord in writing on or before the date the landlord sells or otherwise disposes of the personal property form the dwelling unit or the place of safekeeping, the tenant has five days to reclaim the personal property.   To reclaim the personal property the tenant must only pay the landlord for the cost of removal and storage for the period the tenant's personal property remained in the landlord's safekeeping.   The tenant is allowed a one-time entry to recover personal papers related to employment, medical records, etc.

h.   In this section "abandonment" means the absence of the tenant from the dwelling unit, without notice to the landlord for at least seven days, if rent for the dwelling unit is outstanding and unpaid for ten days and there is no reasonable evidence other than the presence of the tenant's personal property that the tenant is occupying the residence or if there is no evidence of personal property in the unit, then five days after posting the notice the landlord may enter.

Section A.R.S. 33-1370 has been completely rewritten and for the first time the landlord has definitive guidelines for dealing with abandoned property. It is highly recommended that the landlord follow the guidelines set forth in this section.

1. *Send the tenant a notice of abandonment by certified mail, return receipt requested, addressed to the tenant's last known address and any alternative addresses known. (i.e., employment ,family, etc.),*

2. *Post the notice of abandonment on the tenant's door or any other conspicuous place and,*

3. *Wait 5 days after mailing and posting the notice before retaking the premises. Locks should be changed.*

Reasonable care must be used in holding a tenant's property. If the tenant makes no reasonable effort to claim the property, the landlord may sell it and apply the proceeds to any outstanding rent. Only if provided in the lease can the landlord destroy or dispose of property that has little or no value without holding it for the requisite twenty-one day period.

It is till imperative that a landlord believes a tenant has abandoned the property, that the landlord take any of the following steps in addition to posting the notice on the tenant's door and mailing a copy Certified or Registered mail. 1) The landlord should contact neighbors, the tenant's last known employer, and any reference names listed on the tenant's lease or application. 2) Inquire whether or not they have knowledge of the tenant's whereabouts. 3) The landlord should also properly enter the residence and determine whether or not the tenant is still living in the dwelling. The landlord should look for such things as stale food in the refrigerator, lack of clothing or other personal items, or the removal of furniture by tenant. All of the above should be documented in notes taken by the landlord and retained in the tenant's file.

(See humorous example pg. 48)

Waiver of Landlord's Right to Terminate
(A.R.S. Section 33-1371)

Acceptance of rent, or/and portion thereof, with knowledge of a default by tenant constitutes a wavier of his right to terminate the rental agreement for that breach, unless otherwise agreed in writing by the tenant after the breach has occurred. For instance, the landlords accepts a partial payment of rent after given a 5-day notice for nonpayment of rent, the landlord has no right to begin court action to evict the tenant unless the tenant signs an agreement that the partial payment does not void the landlord's right to proceed or until after the landlord has given the tenant a new 5-day notice for the balance of the rent that is due. A landlord is not required to accept a partial payment of rent at any time. If a landlord does accept a partial payment, it must be with a signed wavier agreement.

The landlord may also use a non-waiver agreement after court action and a judgment has been entered against the tenant. Therefore, if the landlord wishes to let the tenant make payments and remain in the property and the tenant defaults in those payments, the landlord may have the Constable remove the tenant through a Writ of Restitution without further notice or further action.

Landlord Liens, Distrait for Rent *(A.R.S. Section 33-1372)*

a.   A lien or security interest on behalf of the landlord in the tenant's household goods is not enforceable. The landlord cannot hold a tenant's property in an effort to force the tenant to pay for their rent.

b.   Distrait for rent is abolished. A landlord cannot change locks or prevent a tenant from having access to their dwelling unit even if the tenant is in default of the rental agreement.

Remedy after Termination *(A.R.S. Section 33-1373)*

If the rental agreement is terminated, the landlord may have a claim for possession and for the rent, the landlord may also bring a separate claim for actual damage for breach of the rental agreement (i.e., (1) unpaid rent due from the date the tenant moves out until the property is re-rented or the term of the rental agreement expires, whichever comes first, and (2) any physical damage to the dwelling unit caused by the tenant, normal wear excepted).

(See humorous example pg. 49)

Recovery of Possession Limited *(A.R.S. Section 33-1374)*

A landlord may not recover or take possession of the dwelling unit by action or otherwise, including willful diminution of services to the tenant by interruption or causing the interruption of electric, gas, water, or other essential service to the tenant, except in case of abandonment, surrender or as permitted by law.

Landlord and Tenant Remedies for Abuse of Access
(A.R.S. Section 33-1376)

a.   If the tenant refuses to allow lawful access, the landlord may obtain injunctive relief through court to compel access, or terminate the rental agreement. In either case, the landlord may recover actual damages.

b.   If the landlord makes an unlawful entry or a lawful entry in an unreasonable manner or make repeated demands for entry otherwise lawful but which have the effect of unreasonably harassing the tenant, the tenant may obtain injunctive relief to prevent the recurrence of the conduct or terminate the rental agreement. In either case, the tenant may recover actual damages not less than an amount equal to one month's rent.

Should the tenant refuse to allow the landlord to enter after proper notice, the landlord should deliver a written notice to the tenant advising the tenant that the landlord intends to terminate the rental agreement effective immediately. The landlord then may file a Forcible Detainer action to remove the tenant from the property. If the tenant believes the landlord is abusing its right of entry, the tenant should also deliver a written notice to the landlord advising the landlord that the tenant is terminating the rental agreement and wants its security deposit back. It is very difficult to obtain monetary damages under this section as the tenant must be able to show that in some way they have been damaged by the landlord's abuse of access.

(See humorous example pg. 49)

AND HERE'S THE BATHROOM

Landlord's Rights

Noncompliance with Rental Agreement by Tenant; Failure to Pay Rent *(A.R.S. Section 33-1368)*

a. Except as provided in this chapter, if there is a material noncompliance by the tenant with the rental agreement, the landlord may deliver a written notice to the tenant specifying the acts and omissions constituting the breach and that the rental agreement will terminate upon a date not less than ten days after receipt of the notice if the breach is not remedied in ten days. If there is a noncompliance by the tenant with Section 33-1341 materially affecting health and safety, the landlord may deliver a written notice to the tenant specifying the acts and omissions constituting the breach and that the rental agreement will terminate upon a date not less than five days after receipt of the notice if the breach is not remedied in five days. However, if the breach is remediable by repair or the payment of damages or otherwise, and the tenant adequately remedies the breach prior to the date specified in the notice, the rental agreement will not terminate. If there is an additional act of these types of noncompliances of the same or similar nature with the remainder of the tenancy from the previous remedy of noncompliance, the landlord may institute a special detainer action pursuant to Section 33-1377 ten days after delivery of a written notice advising the tenant that a second noncompliance of the same or similar nature has occurred. If there is any material falsification by the tenant regarding employment, income, pets or occupants, this may constitute a material noncompliance. If the tenant falsifies information

16

regarding prior evictions, criminal history or current criminal activity, the landlord need only give a ten-day notice to move. If there is a breach that is both material and irreparable, such as an illegal discharge of a weapon on the premises or infliction of serious bodily harm on the landlord, his agent, or another tenant, threatening or intimidating as defined in Section 13-1202 or assault as defined in Section 13-1203 of the landlord or other tenants, or involving imminent serious property damages or any criminal activity, the landlord may deliver a written notice for immediate termination of the rental agreement and shall proceed under Section 33-1377.

In Section a. (above), as with A.R.S. Section 33-1361 the notice for a material noncompliance is now a 10-day notice and the notice for the health and safety violations is 5-days. Again, written notice itemizing the violations must be delivered in hand or sent certified/registered mail.

The legislature has further clarified the landlord's legal position in respect to numerous tenant noncompliance violations of a similar nature that occur over an extensive period of time. If there are additional acts of noncompliance during the tenancy from the previous remedy, the landlord can institute a special detainer action pursuant to A.R.S. 33-1377 and after 10 days notice to the tenant of the second violation of noncompliance

A.R.S. Section 33-1368a enlarges the grounds upon which the landlord can evict a tenant immediately for a breach that is material and irreparable. In addition to the examples of discharging a weapon or inflicting serious bodily harm, the statute now includes acts involving imminent serious property damage and serious acts that threaten or intimidate the landlord, his agents or other tenants. The threats or intimidation must be comparable to those that would fall within the criminal statutes. What will be sufficient grounds to evict a tenant under this section will be left to a judge's determination of the particular facts involved. Most importantly if the tenant is found guilty under this section the court can issue a Writ of Restitution against the tenant to vacate the premises within 12-24 hours of the court hearing, instead of giving the tenant the additional 5 days to move.

b. If rent is unpaid when due and the tenant fails to pay rent within five days after written notice by the landlord of nonpayment and his intention to terminate the rental agreement if the rent is not paid within that period of time, the landlord may terminate the rental agreement by filing a special detainer action pursuant to Section 33-1377. Prior to the filing of a special detainer action, the rental agreement shall be reinstated if the tenant tender all past due and unpaid period rent, and a reasonable late fee is set forth in a written rental agreement. After a special detainer action is filed, the rental agreement is reinstated only if the tenant pays all past due rent, reasonable late fee set forth in a written rental agreement, attorney fees and court costs.

   c.   The landlord may recover all reasonable damages resulting from noncompliance by the tenant with the rental agreement or Section 33-1341 or occupancy of the dwelling unit, court costs, reasonable attorney fees, and all quantifiable damages caused by the tenant to the premises.

   In Section c. A.R.S. Section 33-1368 now gives the court discretion to additionally award the landlord all reasonable damages (and attorney fees) incurred. The damages must be quantifiable, that is easily calculated and not estimated, with supporting documentation.

   The landlord may now discontinue utility services provided by the landlord the day after the Constable serves a Writ of Restitution on the tenant. Disconnections must be performed only by a person authorized by the utility company whose service is being disconnected. If the tenant pays for his own utilities then the landlord may not use this section to disconnect a tenant's utilities. Under no circumstances should the landlord ever disconnect a tenant's utilities without permission from the Constable or Sheriff.

   d.   The landlord shall hold the tenant's personal property for a period of ten days beginning on the first day after a Writ of Restitution or Writ of Execution is executed as prescribed in Section 12-1181. The landlord shall use reasonable care in moving and holding the tenant's property and may store the tenant's property in an unoccupied dwelling unit owned by the landlord or off the premises if an unoccupied dwelling unit is not available. The landlord shall prepare an inventory and promptly notify the tenant of the location and cost of storage of the personal property by sending a notice by certified mail, return receipt requested, addressed to the tenant's last know address and to any of the tenant's alternative addresses known to the landlord. To reclaim the personal property, the tenant shall pay the landlord only for the cost of removal and storage for the time the property is held by the landlord. Again, the tenant may enter one time to reclaim necessary business or personal papers. If the landlord holds the property for the ten day period and the tenant does not make a reasonable effort to recover it, the landlord, upon the expiration of ten days as provide in this subsection, may administer the personal property as provided in Section 33-1370, Subsection E. The landlord shall hold personal property after a Writ of Restitution or Writ of Execution is executed for not more than ten days after such an execution.

This section is the most used by landlords to evict tenants from the premises. It is very important that the proper written notice be delivered to the tenant and that the time periods expire prior to the landlord filing a court action to evict the tenant. It is often an objective determination on the part of the landlord as to what is a noncompliance. The landlord should always have witnesses ready to appear in court who have personal knowledge of the tenant's noncompliance. What is health and safety noncompliance as opposed to a material noncompliance is difficult to determine. Normally, the health and safety noncompliance goes to the more serious violations. Additionally, care should be used in giving the tenant an immediate termination notice for a material and irreparable breach. The courts limit these types of notices to the most serious violations, which include discharge of a weapon, destruction of property, criminal activity or serious infliction of bodily injury. Mere verbal threats normally are not enough to justify use of this type of notice unless they are threats of bodily harm or damage to property.

Failure to Maintain *(A.R.S. Section 33-1369)*

If there is noncompliance by the tenant with A.R.S. Section 33-1341 (*see Tenant's Obligations*) materially affecting health and safety that can be remedied by repair, replacement or a damaged item, or cleaning and the tenant fails to comply as promptly as conditions required in case of emergency or within fourteen days after written notice by the landlord specifying the breach and after written notice by the landlord specifying the breach and requesting that the tenant remedy it within the period of time, the landlord may enter the dwelling unit and cause the work to be done in a workmanlike manner and submit an itemized bill for the actual and reasonable costs or the fair and reasonable value thereof as rent on the next date when periodic rent is due, or if the rental agreement has terminated, for immediate payment.

This section should only be used if the tenant does damages to the property. The landlord may give the tenant the 14-day notice to make the repairs, and if the repairs are not made then the landlord may enter and have those repairs done. The landlord then should give the tenant a bill itemizing the cost of the repairs and a notice that these must be paid with the next rental payment. If the tenant fails to pay rent plus these additional repairs, then the landlord may give the tenant a 7-day notice and proceed through the Forcible Detainer eviction action.

TENANTS HAVE RIGHTS TOO !

Tenant's Rights

Noncompliance by the Landlord *(A.R.S. Section 33-1361)*

a. Except as provided in this chapter, if there is a material noncompliance by the landlord with the rental agreement, the tenant may deliver a written notice to the landlord specifying the acts and omissions constituting the breach and that the rental agreement will terminate upon a date not less than ten days after receipt of the notice if the breach is not remedied in those ten days. If there is a noncompliance by the landlord with Section 33-1324 materially affecting health and safety, the tenant may deliver a written notice to the landlord specifying the acts and omissions constituting the breach and that the rental agreement will terminate upon a date not less than five days after receipt of the notice if the breach is not remedied in the five days. The rental agreement shall terminate and the dwelling unit shall be vacated as provided in the notice subject to the following.

> **1.** If the breach is remediable by repairs or the payment of damages or otherwise and the landlord adequately remedies the breach prior to the date specified in the notice, the rental agreement will not terminated.
>
> **2.** The tenant may not terminate for a condition caused by the deliberate or negligent act or omission of the tenant, a

member of his family, or other person on the premises with his consent.

3. If the landlord falsifies services or conditions of the apartment in writing, the tenant can also give a noncompliance notice to correct those.

b. Except as provided in this chapter, the tenant may recover damages and obtain injunctive relief for any noncompliance by the landlord with the rental agreement or Section 33-1324.

c. The remedy provided in subsection B of this section is in addition to any right of the tenant arising under subsection A of this section.

d. If the rental agreement is terminated, the landlord shall return all security recoverable by the tenant under Section 33-1321. (*See Security Deposits.*)

Remember, the notice should be in writing and delivered in hand by the tenant or sent registered or certified mail.

1. If the breach is remediable by repairs or the payment of damages or otherwise and the landlord adequately remedies the breach prior to the date specified in the notice, the rental agreement will not terminate.

2. The tenant may not terminate for a condition caused by the deliberate or negligent act or omission of the tenant, a member of his family, or other person on the premise with his consent.

e. The tenant may recover damages and obtain injunctive relief for any noncompliance by the landlord with the rental agreement or A.R.S. Section 33-1324 (*see Landlord's Legal Obligations*) in addition to having the deficiency remedied.

f. If the rental agreement is terminated, the landlord shall return all security recoverable by the tenant under A.R.S. Section 33-1321 (*see Security Deposits*).

This section is almost identical to the landlord's noncompliance section. It is essential that the tenant give the landlord written notice and specify the repairs that need to be done or the written representations of the apartment complex the tenant feels are false. General cosmetic type repairs are not authorized under this section. The repairs should pertain to the health and safety or the more serious violations by the landlord. If the tenant is making telephone calls or verbally communicating their requests for repairs, it is advisable that the tenant keep a diary or log of these calls. But always follow up with written notice.

Failure to Deliver Possession *(A.R.S. Section 33-1362)*

a.   If the landlord fails to deliver physical possession of the dwelling unit to the tenant on the date agreed when the rental agreement is to begin, rent abates until possession is delivered and the tenant may do either of the following:

> **1.**   Upon at least five days' written notice to the landlord terminate the rental agreement. Upon termination the landlord shall return all prepaid rent and security.
>
> **2.**   Demand performance of the rental agreement by the landlord, and if the tenant elects, maintain an action for possession of the dwelling unit against the landlord or any person wrongfully in possession and recover the damages sustained by him *(see Forcible Entry and Detainer)*.

b.   If the landlord fails to deliver possession to the tenant because of noncompliance with A.R.S. Section 33-1324 *(see Landlord's Legal Obligations)*, rent shall not abate. Tenant may proceed with the remedies provided for in A.R.S. Section 33-1361 *(see Noncompliance by Landlord)*.

c.   If the landlord's failure to deliver possession is willful and not in good faith, the aggrieved person may recover from that person an amount not more than two month's periodic rent or twice the actual damages sustained by him, whichever is greater.

Self-Help for Minor Defects *(A.R.S. Section 33-1363)*

a.   If the landlord fails to comply with Section 33-1324, and the reasonable cost of compliance is less than three hundred dollars, or an amount equal to one-half of the monthly rent, whichever amount is greater, the tenant may recover damages from the breach under Section 33-1361, subsection B, or may notify the landlord of his intention to correct the condition at the landlord's expense. After being notified by the tenant in writing, if the landlord fails to comply within ten days or as promptly thereafter as conditions require in case of emergency, the tenant may cause the work to be done by a licensed contractor and, after submitting to the landlord an itemized statement and a waiver of lien, deduct from his rent the actual and reasonable cost of the work, not exceeding the amount specified in this subsection.

b.   A tenant may not repair at the landlords' expense if the condition was caused by the deliberate or negligent act or omission of the tenant, a member of his family, or other person on the premises with his consent.

c.   This is one of the few sections that allows a tenant to deduct amounts from their rent payments, so long as the tenant follows all steps set forth in Section A.

It is also crucial that the tenant follow this section to the letter. The tenant must give the proper written notice, must use a licensed contractor, and must submit an itemized statement and lien waiver in order to deduct the costs of the repair from their rent. Also, the deductions are limited to $300.00 or one half of one month's rent, whichever is greater.

Wrongful Failure to Supply Heat, Air Conditioning, Cooling, Water, Hot Water, or Essential Services
(A.R.S. Section 33-1364)

a.   If contrary to the rental agreement or A.R.S. Section 33-1324 (*see Landlord's Legal Obligations*) the landlord deliberately or negligently fails to supply running water, hot water or heat, air-conditioning or cooling, where such units are installed or offered, or essential service, the tenant may give reasonable notice to the landlord specifying the breach and may do one of the following:

1.   Procure reasonable amounts of hot water, heat, and essential services during the period of the landlord's noncompliance and deduct their actual reasonable cost from the rent. If the landlord supplies utilities and these utilities are to be shut off for nonpayment, the tenant may negotiate with the utility company to pay for the utility and then deduction that cost from their rent.

2.   Recover damages based upon the diminution in the fair rental value of the dwelling unit.

3.   Procure reasonable substitute housing (i.e., rent a motel room) during the period of the landlord's noncompliance, in which case the tenant is excused from paying rent for the prior of the landlord's noncompliance. In the event the periodic cost of such substitute housing exceeds the amount of the periodic rent, upon delivery by tenant of proof of payment for such substitute housing, tenant may recover from the landlord such excess costs up to an amount not to exceed twenty-five percent of the periodic rent which has been excused pursuant to this paragraph.

b.   In the event the landlord's noncompliance is deliberate, the tenant may also recover the actual and reasonable cost of fair and reasonable value of the substitute housing not in excess of an amount equal to the periodic rent.

    c. If the tenant proceeds under this section, he may not proceed under A.R.S. Section 33-1361 or 33-1363 *(see Remedies)* as to that breach.

    d. The rights under this section do not arise until the tenant has given notice to the landlord and such rights do not include the right to repair. Such rights do not arise if the condition was caused by the deliberate or negligent act or omission of the tenant, a member of his family, or other person on the premises with his consent. What is reasonable notice by the tenant, and whether or not the condition was caused by the deliberate or negligent actions of the landlord, depends on the facts of each situation. The landlord, however, can disconnect or shut off utilities to make needed repairs without any compensation to the tenant.

It is also crucial under this section that the tenant notify the landlord in writing. This section most often arises in air conditioning units that become defective during the hot summer months or heating units which become defective during the winter months. In order for the tenant to use this section, the tenant must show that the landlord either deliberately or negligently failed to supply the essential services. This can often be difficult if a landlord is taking all reasonable steps to have the problem fixed. Some inconvenience always accompanies a repair problem concerning essential services and the tenants are expected to incur a limited amount of discomfort, but not discomfort that affects their health and safety. (See humorous example pg. 50)

Landlord's Noncompliance as Defense to Action for Possession or Rent *(A.R.S. Section 33-1365)*

    a. In an action for possession upon nonpayment of the rent or in an action for rent where the tenant is in possession, the tenant may counterclaim for any amount which he may recover under the rental agreement or the Landlord Tenant Act. In that event after notice and hearing the court may order the tenant to pay into court all or part of the undisputed rent accrued and all periodic rent thereafter accruing and shall determine the amount due to each party.

    b. In an action for rent where the tenant is not in possession, the tenant may counterclaim but is not required to pay any rent into court.

    c. A tenant can only countersue for damages allegedly suffered that arise out of the rental agreement or the Landlord and Tenant Act. For instance, a tenant who had separately agreed to clean or repair other apartments for the landlord would have to file a separate lawsuit against the landlord for breach of contract. If the tenant wishes to invoke this provision of the law, they must be prepared to pay their rent into court at the time of their eviction hearing. They must also be prepared to have filed a written countersuit, itemizing their damages and the reasons they believe they are entitled to some type of monetary relief. They should always deliver a copy of the countersuit as quickly as possible to their landlord, so that the landlord has notice of what the claim is. It is essentially illegal in Arizona to withhold your rent because a landlord fails or inadequately makes repairs. The court's reasoning is that if a tenant withholds their rent because of a failure to make repairs, then the tenant has the rent money available and should be able to deposit that with the court. *(See humorous example pg. 50)*

Fire or Casualty Damage *(A.R.S. Section 33-1366)*

a.   If the dwelling unit or premises are damaged or destroyed by fire or casualty to an extent that enjoyment of the dwelling unit is substantially impaired, the tenant may do either of the following:

> **1.**   Immediately vacate the premises and notify the landlord in writing within fourteen days thereafter of his intention to terminate the rental agreement, in which case the rental agreement terminates as of the date of vacating.
>
> **2.**   If continued occupancy is lawful, vacate any party of the dwelling unit rendered unusable by the fire or casualty, in which case the tenant's liability of rent is reduced in proportion to the diminution in the fair rental value of the dwelling unit.

b.   If the rental agreement is terminated, the landlord shall return all security recoverable under A.R.S. Section 33-1321 *(see Security Deposits)*.

Tenant's Remedies for Landlord's Unlawful Ouster, Exclusion or Diminution of Services *(A.R.S. Section 33-1367)*

If the landlord unlawfully removes or excludes the tenant from the premises or willfully diminishes services to the tenant by interrupting or causing the interruption of electric, gas, water or other essential service to the tenant, the tenant may recover possession or terminate the rental agreement and, in either case, recover an amount not more than two months' periodic rent or twice the actual damages sustained by him, whichever is greater. If the rental agreement is terminated, the landlord shall return all security recoverable under A.R.S. Section 33-1321 (*See Security Deposits*).

Discrimination and Minors

Discrimination by Landlord or Lessor Against Tenant with Children is Prohibited *(A.R.S. Section 33-1317)*

a.   A person who knowingly refuses to rent to any other person a place to be used for a dwelling for the reason that the other person has a child or children, or who advertises in connection with the rental a restriction against children, either by display of sign, placard, written or printed notice, or by a publication thereof in a newspaper of general circulation, is guilty of a petty offense. There is a range of fines and assessment of damages, attorney fees and costs, and it is a criminal offense in Arizona. Child is defined as any person under 18 years of age.

b.   Generally a rental agreement entered into between a minor and an adult may be voiced (cancelled) by the minor but is binding on the adult and cannot be cancelled. However, if the dwelling unit is a necessity for the minor (i.e., he or she is emancipated and not dependent upon parents or resents his or her age and leads the landlord to believe the minor is an adult), the landlord may terminate the rental agreement because of fraud or misrepresentation

c.   A landlord can set a reasonable occupancy standard for the number of people that can occupy an apartment. Two people per bedroom is presumed reasonable. However, such factors as square footage, facilities, parking, etc. should be taken into account.

In addition to the state statute, the federal government enacted a new discrimination law in March of 1989. The new law is entitled "The Fair Housing Amendments Act of 1988". Federal law prohibits discrimination in the sale, rental and financing of dwellings based on color, religion, sex or national origin. The Fair Housing Amendments Act expands the coverage to prohibit discriminatory housing practices based on a handicap and family status. There are some very severe fines which the federal government can impose upon a landlord found guilty of violating this Act. Arizona also has its own separate Fair Housing law.

Notice

Notice *(A.R.S. Section 33-1313)*

a.   A person has notice of a fact if he has actual knowledge of it, has received a notice or notification of it, or from all the facts and circumstances known to him at the time in question, he has reason to know that it exists. A person "knows" or has knowledge of a fact if he has actual knowledge of it.

b.   A person "notifies" or gives a notice or notification to another by taking steps reasonably calculated to inform the other in ordinary course whether or not the other actually comes to know of it. A person "receives" a notice or notification when it comes to his attention, or in the case of the landlord, it has been delivered in hand or mailed by registered or certified mail to the place of business of the landlord through which the rental agreement was made, or at any place held out by him as the place for receipt of the communication or delivered to any individual who is designated as an agent by A.R.S. Section 33-1322 (see Moving In), or in the case of the tenant, it is delivered in hand to the tenant or mailed by registered or certified mail to him at the place held out by him as the place for receipt of the communication or, in the absence of such designation, to his last known place of resident. If notice is mailed by registered or certified mail, the tenant or landlord is deemed to have such notice on the date the notice is actually received by him, or five days after the date the notice is mailed whichever occurs first.

c.   "Notice," knowledge of a notice or notification received by an organization, is effective for a particular transaction from the time it is brought to the attention of the individual conducting the transaction and in any event from the time it would have been brought to his attention if the organization had exercised reasonable diligence.

d.   While it is possible to deliver notices to the dwelling unit by slipping them under the door, or posting them on the door, it is always recommended the notice be personally delivered, or sent registered or certified mail. That way, there is no question about receipt. However, if a notice is not personally delivered, always "follow up" by contacting the person later that day, or the next day, to make sure they received it.

e.   The most common types of notices given are as follows:

   1.   5-day notice for nonpayment of rent. The notice must tell tenant if all rent is not paid within five days, the landlord may terminate the rental agreement and bring an action to evict the tenant.

2. Noncompliance notices. These give either the landlord or the tenant ten days to correct a problem (i.e., loud noise, unauthorized guests in the apartment, abandoned or junk vehicles, etc.) and if not corrected within ten days, the rental agreement will terminate on the 10th days from the date of the notice. Alternatively, five days to correct a problem dealing with health and safety or the rental agreement terminates 5 days from receipt of the notice.

3. Immediate termination of the rental agreement for material and irreparable breaches (i.e., discharge of a weapon, physical assault, damage, or destruction to the dwelling unit).

4. 30-day notice to terminate the rental agreement or change rules and regulations, or in some instances, increase the rent.

5. 5-day notice to vacate to trespassers, unauthorized guests, or on-site employees who have been terminated.

6. 12-day written notice that a check (usually for the rent) has been dishonored by a bank and if not made good within twelve days the writer of the check will be liable for double its amount or $50, whichever is greater.

7. 2-day access notice informing a tenant when the landlord will enter the dwelling unit.
    (See humorous example pg. 51)

Retaliatory Action by the Landlord

Retaliatory Conduct Prohibited *(A.R.S. Section 33-1381)*

a. A landlord may not retaliate by increasing rent or decreasing services or by bringing or threatening to bring an action for possession after any of the following:

1. The tenant has complained to a governmental agency charged with responsibility for enforcement of a building or housing code or a violation applicable to the premises materially affecting health and safety.
2. The tenant has complained to the landlord of a violation under A.R.S. Section 33-1324 (see Landlord's Legal Obligations).
3. The tenant has organized or become a member of a tenant's union or similar organization.
4. The tenant has complained to a governmental agency charged with the responsibility of the wage-price stabilization act.

b. If the landlord acts in violation of subsection A of this section, the tenant is entitled to the remedies provided in A.R.S. Section 33-1367 *(see Tenant's Rights VIII)* and has a defense in an action against him for possession. In an action by or against the tenant, evidence of a complaint within six months prior to the alleged act of retaliation creates a presumption that the landlord's conduct was in retaliation. The presumption does not arise if the tenant made the compliant after notice of termination of the rental agreement. "Presumption" in this subsection means that the trier of fact (judge or jury) must find the existence of the fact presumed unless and until evidence is introduced which would support a finding of its nonexistence. In other words, the landlord must show a valid reason for evicting the tenant (i.e., nonpayment of rent, or noncompliance with the rental agreement).

c. A landlord may bring action for possession if either of the following occurs:

1. The violation of the applicable building or housing code was caused primarily by lack of reasonable care by the tenant or other persons in his household or upon the premises with his consent.
2. The tenant is in default in rent. The maintenance of the action does not release the landlord from liability under A.R.S. Section 33-1361 *(See Tenant's Rights I).*
   (See humorous example pg. 51.)

TOP 10 DO's and DON'T's

DO

1. Inspect the rental house or apartment prior to moving in. Have a written walk through inspection sheet signed by both landlord and tenant.

2. Always get a written rent receipt for rent paid. Pay your rent in person.

3. Any special condition or provision of your lease should be written. Always use written leases and have all adult tenants who will occupy the premises sign the lease.

4. Any repair requests or demand notices from either landlord or tenant must be in writing and either hand-delivered or sent certified or registered mail.

5. Do a walk through together at the expiration of the lease so that the landlord and tenant may agree on the condition of the rental premises.

6. Always give at least 30 days written notice prior to the expiration of the lease if you are going to be moving or not renewing the lease.

7. Always refund a tenant's refundable deposit within 14 business days after the lease ends and demand is made. If none or only a part of the deposit is being refunded itemize all charges beyond normal wear and tear, and have them supported by repair invoices. Tenants should always provide a forwarding address.

8. Always make any repairs that pertain to the health and safety of the rental property or to its habitability.

9. Always timely pay your rent, or if paying late include all appropriate late charges.

10. Always treat any prospective renters the same. Do not discriminate based on race, religion, sex, color, national origin, families or handicapped.

DON'T

1. Never put cash or money orders through the landlord's mail drop.

2. Don't use verbal rental agreements. They are legal but usually end up in "swearing contests" in court. Never agree verbally to do something (reduce it to writing).

3. Never refuse to pay rent or withhold rent to force a landlord to make repairs. Conversely, never refuse to make legitimate repairs even if the tenant is refusing to pay rent.

4. Never just move out leaving the keys in the rental premises or mailing them to the landlord.

5. Do not move out in the middle of your lease. You are legally responsible for the balance of the lease or until the property is re-rented.

6. Never disconnect a tenant's utilities, lock a tenant out of their rental home, or seize a tenant's personal property while the tenant is residing in the premises.

7. If you are a tenant, never make repairs yourself then deduct them from your rent. If you are a landlord, never use unqualified people to make repairs.

8. Whether you are a landlord or tenant, never refuse to give either your current phone number or address.

9. Never falsify information on your rental application or fail to answer all questions completely and thoroughly.

10. Never wait for a court hearing to bring up your complaints. Never refuse to open the lines of communication with each other if a problem exists.

Rental Increase

A landlord may not increase the amount of rental payments during the term of a fixed lease (i.e., 6 months or a year). However, at least 30 days prior to the expiration of the fixed term lease, the landlord may give written notice of a rent increase. If a tenant is not on a fixed term lease (i.e., month to month), then the landlord may increase the monthly rental amount by giving the tenant at least 30 days written notice of the increase. The notice must be that the new increase will take effect no sooner than 30 days from the date when rent is due and payable.

The rent increase should be fair and base, in part, on comparable rental rates for similarly located rental units.

Moving Out

Periodic Tenancy; Holdover Remedies
(A.R.S. Section 33-1375)

a.   The landlord or the tenant may terminate a week-to-week tenancy by a written notice given to the other at least ten days prior to the termination date specified in the notice.

b.   The landlord or the tenant may terminate a month-to-month tenancy by a written notice given to the other at least thirty days prior to the periodic rental date specified in the notice. For instance, if rent is due on the first of every month, then the termination notice must be given at least 30 days prior to the date rent is due.

c.   If the tenant remains in possession without the landlord's consent after expiration of the term of the rental agreement or its termination, the landlord may bring an action for possession (forcible entry and detainer) and if the tenant's holdover is willful and not in good faith, the landlord in addition may recover an amount equal to not more than two months' periodic rent or twice the actual damages sustained by him, whichever is greater. Remember the rights and duties regarding security deposits and their return, or application to damages. It is always recommended that landlord and tenant inspect the property together on move-out, and if necessary, have witnesses present and take photographs.

If the landlord wishes to terminate a month-to-month tenancy or a lease that is about to expire, the landlord should give 30 days written notice to the tenants at least 30 days from the rental due date. For instance, if the rent is due on the first of the month and the landlord gives the tenant a 30 day notice on the fourth of the month, that notice would not be effective until the end of the next month. On the other hand, if the tenant gives the landlord a 30 day notice that they are going to move out and then changes their mind, the landlord may hold the tenant to that notice and at the end of the 30 days notice period immediately bring an eviction action to remove the tenant plus ask for the two months' rent as damages. In order to avoid damages for holding over, a tenant must show a compelling reason for not moving (i.e., serious medical problems).

Forcible Entry and Detainer (Eviction)

Acts Which Constitute Forcible Entry or Detainer
(A.R.S. Section 12-1171)

A person is guilty of forcible entry and detainer or of forcible detainer as the case may be if he:

1. Makes an entry into any lands, tenements or other real property without permission.
2. Makes such an entry by force.
3. Willfully and without force holds over any lands, tenements or real property after termination of the time for which such lands, tenements or other real property were let to him or to the person under whom he claims, after demand made in writing for the possession thereof by the person entitled to such possession.

Definition of Forcible Entry *(A.R.S. Section 12-1172)*

A "forcible entry", or an entry where entry is not given by law within the meaning of this articles, is:

1. An entry without the consent of the person having the actual possession.
2. As to a landlord, an entry upon his property without his consent.

Definition of Forcible Detainer; Substitution of Parties
(A.R.S. Section 12-1173)

There is a forcible detainer if:

1. A tenant at will or by sufferance, or a tenant from month to month or a lesser period whose tenancy has been terminated, retains possession after his tenancy has been terminated or after he receives written demand of possession by the landlord.
2. The tenant of a person who has made a forcible entry refuses for five days after written demand to give possession to the person upon whose possession the forcible entry was made.
3. A person who had made a forcible entry upon the possession of one who acquired such possession by forcible entry refuses for five days after written demand to give possession to the person upon whose possession the first forcible entry was made.
4. A person who has made a forcible entry upon the possession of a tenant for a term refuses to deliver possession to the landlord for five days after written demand, after the term expires. If the term expires while a writ of forcible entry applied for by the tenant is pending, the landlord may, at his own cost and for his own benefit, prosecute it is the name of the tenant.

Additional Definition of Forcible Detainer
(A.R.S. Section 12-1173.01)

a. In addition to the other persons enumerated in this article, a person in any of the following cases who retains possession of any land, tenements or other real property after he receives written demand of possession may be removed through an action for forcible detainer filed with the Clerk of the Superior Court in accordance with this article:

1. If the property has been sold through the foreclosure of a mortgage, deed of trust, or contract for conveyance of real property.
2. If the property has been sold through a trustee's sale under a deed of trust.
3. If the property has been forfeited through a contract for conveyance of real property.
4. If the property has been sold by virtue of an execution and the

title has been duly transferred.

5. If the property has been sold by the owner and the title has been duly transferred.

b.   The remedies provided in this section do not affect the rights of persons in possession under a lease or other possessory right which is superior to the interest sold, forfeited, or executed upon.

c.   The remedies provided by this section are in addition to and do not preclude any other remedy granted by law.

In essence, the Forcible Entry and Detainer statutes are a legal term for an eviction action. It is simply a name given to the lawsuit which the landlord may bring against the tenant to remove the tenant from the property. Forcible Entry and Detainer may be used against the tenants, trespassers or terminated employees. For instance, if the resident has moved someone into their apartment without permission of the landlord, the landlord may use a Forcible Entry and Detainer action after proper notice to remove the unauthorized guest. If an employee has been given their apartment as part of their compensation for being employed by the landlord and the employee is terminated, the landlord may also use the Forcible Entry and Detainer action, after proper notice, to remove the employee from the property. Additionally, Forcible Detainer may be used after a Trustee's Sale or foreclosure action where a house has been returned to a mortgage company or lender and the prior owner of the house refuses or fails to move out.

Complaint and Answer; Service and Return
(A.R.S. Section 12-1175)

a.   After proper notice has been given and the tenant has failed to comply with the notice, the landlord may file a complaint of forcible entry or detainer, in writing and under oath, with the Clerk of the Superior Court or a Justice of the Peace. A summons shall immediately issue commanding the person, against whom the complaint is made, to appear in court and answer the complaint at a time and place named. The trial shall be set no more than 5 judicial or court days after the forcible detainer complaint is filed with the Court.

b.   The complaint shall contain a description of the premises or which possession is claimed in sufficient detail to identify them and shall also state the facts which entitle plaintiff to possession and authorize the action (i.e., address of the property and reasons for the eviction).

c.   The summons shall be served at least two days before the return day, and return made thereof on the day assigned for trial. In other words, the forcible detainer papers must be served on the tenant at least two days before the court hearing. Only a license process server may serve the papers.

d.   You have the option of filing your action in either Justice Court or Superior Court. Justice Court has monetary limitations of $10,000 per month rent and $10,000 in rent due. Superior Court has no monetary limits.

Special Detainer Actions
(A.R.S. Section 33-1377)

Special Detainer Actions; Services; Trial Postponement
(A.R.S. Section 33-1377)

a.   Special detainer actions shall be instituted for remedies prescribed in Section 33-1368. Except as provide in this section, the procedure and appeal rights prescribed in Title 12, Chapter 8, Article 4 apply to special detainer actions.

b.   The summons shall be issued on the day the compliance is filed and shall command the person against whom the complaint is made to appear and answer the complaint at the time and place named not more than six nor less than three days from the date of the summons. The tenant is deemed to have received the summons three days after the summons is mailed if personal service is attempted and within one day of issuance of the summons. A copy of the summons is conspicuously posted on the main entrance of the tenant's resident and on the same day the summons is sent certified mail, return receipt requested, to the tenant's last known address. The summons in a special detainer action shall be served at least two days before the return day and the return day made on the day assigned for trial. Service of process by posting and mailing is treated the same as personal service and money judgment are awarded by the courts.

c.   For good cause shown supported by an affidavit, the trial may be postponed for not more than three days in a Justice Court or five days in the Superior Court.

d.   In addition to determining the right to actual possession, the court may assess damages, attorney fees, and costs as prescribed by law.

e.   If a complaint is filed alleging a material and irreparable breach pursuant to Section 33-1368, subsection A, the summons shall be issued as provided in subsection B of this section, except that the trial date and return date shall be set no later than the third day following the filing of the complaint. If after the hearing the court finds that the material and irreparable breach did occur, the court shall order restitution in favor of the plaintiff not less than twelve nor more than twenty-four hours later. The burden of proof is only preponderance of the evidence (fifty-one percent (51%) probability it occurred).

f. If the defendant is found guilty, the court shall give judgment for the plaintiff for restitution of the premises, for late charges stated in the rental agreement, and for costs and, at the plaintiff's option, for all rent found to be due and unpaid through the current periodic rental date and shall grant a Writ of Restitution. Late charges and attorney's fees can also be awarded.

g. If the defendant is found not guilty, judgment shall be given for the defendant against the plaintiff for costs, and if it appears that the plaintiff has acquired possession of the premises since commencement of the action, a Writ of Restitution shall issue in favor of the defendant.

The landlord should specify in the forcible detainer complaint each and every item of damage they are claiming, including unpaid rent and damages to the property. If the tenant requests a jury trial, some of the courts require the tenant to pay jury fees prior to the trial date. Additionally, the losing party will be responsible for all jury fees.

Under special detainer A.R.S. Section 33-1377, it is recommended that this procedure of posting and mailing only be used when the tenant cannot be personally served.

(See humorous example pg. 52)

FEE? I THOUGHT YOU SAID FREE!

Going to Court/Summons; Trial Procedure

Demand for Jury; Trial Procedure *(A.R.S. Section12-1176)*

Either party may request that the case be tried to a jury rather than the judge. However, the party who loses must pay the costs and fees of the jury. The request for a jury trial must be made when the tenant first appears in court.

(See humorous example pg. 43)

Trial and Issue; Postponement of Trial
(A.R.S. Section 12-1177)

a. On the trial of an action of forcible detainer or forcible entry, the only issue the court can determine shall be the right of actual possession, rent due, costs, and attorney's fees, if any.

b. The finding of the court or the jury shall be either guilty or non guilty.

c. For good cause shown, supported by affidavit, the trial may be postponed for a time not to exceed three days in a Justice Court or ten days in a Superior Court.

d.   Counterclaims are not allowed except as stated in Tenant's Rights VI. *(See humorous example pg. 52)*

Judgment; Writ of Restitution; Limitation on Issuance
(A.R.S. Section 12-1178)

a.   If defendant is found guilty, the court shall give judgment for plaintiff for restitution of the premises and for costs and, at plaintiff's option, for all rent found due and unpaid through the current periodic rental period at the date of the judgment, attorney's fee, if any, and shall grant a Writ of Restitution (an order restoring possession of the property to the landlord).

b.   If the defendant is found not guilty, judgment shall be given for defendant against plaintiff for costs and attorney's fee, if any, and if it appears that plaintiff has acquired possession of the premises since commencement of the action, a Writ of Restitution shall issue in favor of defendant restoring the property.

c.   No Writ of Restitution shall issue until the expiration of five days after the rendition of judgment. This is five straight days. If the tenant fails to vacate within the time period, the court can order the Sheriff or Constable to allow the landlord to change locks and remove any property from the premises. The constable is to serve the Writ of Restitution upon the tenant as promptly and expeditiously as possible. Normally, the Writ of Restitution will be served within 2 to 3 days after filing with the Court.

(See humorous example pg. 52)

Appeal to Superior Court; Notice; Bond
(A.R.S. Section 12-1179)

a.   Either party may appeal from a Justice Court to the Superior Court of the county in which the Judgment is given by giving notice as in other civil actions within five days after rendition of the Judgment pursuant to this section. Any motion filed by the tenant will not stop the five-day appeal time.

b.   A party seeking to appeal a Judgment shall file with the Notice of Appeal a bond for costs on appeal, which shall be in an amount set by the Justice of the Peace sufficient to cover the costs on appeal. The bond shall be payable to the Clerk of the Superior Court. If a party is unable to file a bond for costs on appeal, the party shall file with the Justice Court a Notice of Appeal along with an Affidavit stating that he is unable to give bond for costs on appeal and the reasons therefore. Within five court days after the filing of the Affidavit, any other party may file, in the Justice Court, Objections to the Affidavit. The Justice of the Peace shall hold a hearing on the affidavit and Objections within five court days thereafter. If the Justice Court sustains the Objections, the Appellant shall file, within five court days thereafter, a bond for costs on appeal as provided for in this section or in such lesser amount as ordered by the Justice Court.

c.   A party seeking to appeal a Judgment may stay the execution of either the Judgment for possession or any Judgment for money damages by filing a supersedeas bond. The Justice Court shall hold a hearing on the Motion within five court days after the parties advise the Justice Court of their failure to stipulate on the amount of the bond. The Stay is effective when the supersedeas bond or bonds are filed.

d.   The party seeking to stay the execution of the Judgment for possession shall file a supersedeas bond in the amount of rent accruing from the date of the Judgment until the next periodic rental date, together with costs and attorney's fees, if any. The tenant shall pay to the Clerk of the Superior Court, on or before each periodic rental due date during the pendency of the Appeal, the amount of rent due under the terms of the lease or rental agreement. Such amounts shall be made payable by the Superior Court to the owner, landlord or agent as they accrue to satisfy the amount of periodic rent due under the lease or rental agreement. In all cases where the rent due under the terms of the lease or rental agreement is paid through the office of the Clerk of the Superior Court as set forth in this subsection, the order of the court may include a one-time handling fee in the amount of ten dollars to be paid by the party seeking to stay the execution of the Judgment for possession. In no event shall the amounts paid per month exceed the amount of monthly rent charged by the owner for the premises. Where habitability as provided for in Section 33-1324 and Section 33-1364 has been raised as an affirmative defense by the tenant to the nonpayment of rent or when the tenant has filed a Counter-claim asserting a habitability issue, the Superior Court will retain all money paid under this subsection pending a final Judgment.

e.   If during the pendency of the Appeal the party seeking to stay the execution of the Judgment for possession fails to pay the rent on the periodic rental due date, the party in whose favor a Judgment for possession was issued may move the Superior Court to lift the stay of the execution of the Judgment for possession. The Superior Court shall hear the motion to lift the stay of the execution of the Judgment for possession and release accrued monies, if any, within five court days from the failure of the party to pay the periodic rent due under the terms of the lease or rental agreement.

f.   The party seeking to stay the execution of the Judgment for money damages shall file a supersedeas bond in the amount of the Judgment, together with costs and attorney's fees, if any. The amount of the bond shall be fixed by the Court and payable to the Clerk of the Superior Court.

Stay of Proceedings on Judgment; Record on Appeal
(A.R.S. Section 12-1180)

When the appeal bond is filed and approved, the Justice of the Peace shall stay further proceedings on the Judgment and immediately prepare a transcript of all entries on his docket in the action and transmit it, together with all original papers, to the Clerk of the Superior Court of the county in which the trial was held. If the tenant pays as required, he or she may continue to occupy the property until the appeal is decided by a higher court.

(See humorous example pg. 53)

Trial and Judgment on Appeal; Writ of Restitution
(A.R.S. Section 12-1180)

On trial of the action in the Superior Court, the court will determine again the right of possession and monetary damages and whether a Writ of Restitution will be issued. There is no right to a new trial unless the Justice Court failed to tape record or transcribe the hearing. If the Justice Court has a taped record of the hearing, then the Superior Court rules based upon a transcript of the hearing and legal written briefs due in 30 days after notice of appeal.

Appeal to Supreme Court; Stay and Bond
(A.R.S. Section 12-1182)

a.   In a forcible entry or forcible detainer action originally commenced in the Superior Court, an appeal may be taken to Supreme Court as in other civil actions.

b.   The appeal, if taken by the party in possession of the premises, shall not stay execution of the Judgment unless the Superior Court so orders, and appellant shall file a bond in an amount fixed and approved by the court, conditioned that appellant will prosecute the appeal to effect and will pay the rental value of the premises pending the appeal and all damages, costs and rent adjudged against him by the Superior Court or the

Supreme Court.

(See humorous example pg. 53)

Other court proceedings that are available to residents and tenants are:

    a. If a dispute does not deal with the right of possession (i.e., forcible entry and detainer) either party may bring a civil suit against the other in either Justice Court (limited to claims not exceeding $10,000.00) or Superior Court. Common examples are defamation of character, trespass, false arrest, negligent actions, or conversion of property.

    b. Small Claims Court. These are limited to disputes which do not exceed $2,500.00, attorneys are not allowed to participate, service of the lawsuit may be done by registered or certified mail and most cases take 40-60 days to complete. There is no right of appeal. Most common use of small claims is by tenants who are either not refunded their security deposit within 14 days as prescribed by law, or who dispute the landlord's deductions from their deposit. For more information see A.R.S. Section 22-501 through 22-523.

Top 10 – Going to Court

1. Have your file in order. Have extra copies of ledger cards, notices, letter, photos, invoices for repairs, etc.

2. Have all necessary witnesses available to testify.

3. Do not bring letters, whether or not they are notarized. The witness must be in court. A written statement or letter is hearsay.

4. Review your file with both your witnesses and your attorney, if you have one.

5. If you are not represented by an attorney, consider a consultation with one prior to court.

6. Answer all questions honestly. Do not guess. If you do not recall just say so (i.e., "I do not recall at this time").

7. Keep your answers to questions short and to the point. Some questions call for a yes or no answer. Some questions require an explanation – know the difference.

8. When you appear in court be on time, or better yet be early.

9. Dress appropriately.

10. Once in front of the judge, speak only when you are spoken to. Do not argue or engage in "swearing contests" or "name calling" with your opponent.

General Provisions

The underlying purpose and policies of the Residential Landlord and Tenant Act is to simplify, clarify, modernize, and revise the law governing the rental of dwelling units and the rights and obligations of landlord and tenant and to encourage landlord and tenant to maintain and improve the quality of housing.

Certain situations are excluded, those being:

1. Residence at an institution, public or private, if incidental to detention or the provision of medical, educational, counseling, or religious services.

2. Occupancy under a contract of sale of a dwelling unit if the occupant is the purchaser.

3. Occupancy by a member of a fraternal or social organization in the portion of a structure operated for the benefit of the organization.

4. Transient occupancy in a hotel, motel or recreational lodging.

5. Occupancy by an employee of a landlord as a manager or custodian who right to occupancy is conditional upon employment in and about the premises.

6. Occupancy by owner of a condominium unit or a holder of a proprietary lease in a cooperative.

7. Occupancy in or operation of public housing as authorized by state or federal law.

There is an obligation of good faith on the part of both landlord and tenant in the dealing with each other. In that regard a rental agreement can be reviewed by a court to determine if all of its is unconscionable.

a. If the court, as a matter of law, finds either of the following:

1. A rental agreement or any provision thereof was unconscionable (so unfair or one-sided) when made, the court may refuse to enforce the agreement, enforce the remainder of the agreement without the unconscionable provision, or limit the application of any unconscionable provision to avoid an unconscionable result.

2. A settlement in which a party waives or agrees to forego a claim or right under this chapter or under a rental agreement was unconscionable at the time it was made the court may refuse to enforce the settlement, enforce the remainder of the settlement without the unconscionable provision to void any unconscionable result.

b.   If unconscionability is put into issue by a party or by the court upon its own motion, the parties shall be afforded a reasonable opportunity to present evidence as to the setting, purpose, and effect of the rental agreement or settlement to aid the court in making the determination.

Humorous Examples

Moving In – *Page 1*

The Damned family moves into the Straight Arrow Apartment complex run by manager Prissy Prude. One day, the following people come into Prissy Prude's office and request access to the Damned file. I.R.S. agent Rip U. Off shows proper identification and tells Prissy Prude he is investigating the father, I. L. B. Damned. Child Protective Service Agent Betty Watchout is looking for the mother, U. B. Damned. Process Server, I. V. Gotcha, has a lawsuit to serve on the son, Amster Damned, but does not know his apartment number and has no court order to obtain this information. Finally, Tim A. Date from the Harassment Collection Agency demands to see the Damned file because the daughter, Obie Damned owes a debt on a delinquent account. Prissy allows access to Rip U. Off and Betty Watchout, but not to I. V. Gotcha and Tim A. Date. Prissy says to her assistant manager, "They are looking for the whole Damned family."

Rental Agreement – *Page 3*

Ike and Tina Tenant are referred to the Good Times Apartments by their friends Dick and Pat Nixson, who have retired and are residents at Good Times. Dick and Pat receive a $100.00 referral fee for their referral of Ike and Tina Tenant. Ike and Tina Tenant sign a one year lease and receive a rent concession of $50.00 off of each month's rent if they fulfill all the terms of their lease. A lease addendum is signed so that if Ike and Tina break their lease, management may recover any rent concessions received by Ike and Tina. Ike loses his job after four months and can't pay his rent. Manager Mel Practice delivers a 7-day Notice to Ike and Tina, and files a forcible detainer action in justice court. Ike and Tina argue at court that Mel Practice has no authority to bring the eviction action because he is a manager and not the owner of Good Times, who lives in New York. The case will be dismissed. Ike and Tina file a complaint with the Real Estate Department which begins an investigation into the apartment complex and its management company. Ike and Tina skip out in the middle of the night never to be heard from again. If management could locate Ike and Tina, they could sue them for all rent owed, all rent concessions received, and all rent due under the remainder of the lease (subject to management's duty to use reasonable efforts to re-rent the apartment).

Rules and Regulations – *Page 4*

Manager Trudy Worthless decides to hire Associated Unprofessional Process Servers, Inc. to deliver 5-day Notices to her tenants at the Hurtin' for Certain Apartment Complex. Associated Unprofessional and Trudy agree they will enact a new community policy to charge the tenants $20.00 for the delivery of the 5-day Notices and that Trudy and Associated will split the $20.00 fee when it is collected with the tenant's rent.

Eight months later, tenant Stanford U. Wrights refuses to pay and brings a class action suit on behalf of all the current and former tenants at Hurtin' For Certain Apartment Complex to declare this charge illegal and for reimbursement to all the tenants of all monies collected under this 5-day Notice policy. Judge I. M. Wright (no relationship to Stan) tells Trudy's attorney, the famous Mel Practice, he rules in Stan's favor because the policy violates A.R.S. Section 33-1342(B).

Security Deposits – *Page 7*

Bo Diddley and Bo Jackson rent an apartment from manager Bo Derrick at the Big Ten Apartments. Bo Diddley and Jackson sign a six-month lease and deposit $400.00 as a refundable deposit. Three months later, Bo Diddley loses his job as a back-up musician and Bo Jackson loses his job as a shoe salesman. Bo Jackson and Diddley move out and deliver a letter to Bo Derrick demanding their deposit. Bo Derrick re-rents their apartment a week later but has no forwarding address for her tenants, so mails their deposit less damages to the last known address with a "please forward" on the envelope. The refund has a restrictive endorsement on the back. Three weeks later, Bo Jackson and Diddley get their check, cash it and sue Bo Derrick for the balance due plus double the amount of their original deposit. The case comes before Judge Bo Weevel who dismisses the lawsuit because: 1) The check was chased containing a restrictive endorsement; and 2) The owner was not sued, only Bo Derrick, the manager.

Abandonment – *Page 11*

Betty Bankrupt is evicted by court order but vacates before the Constable can serve a Writ of Restitution. Betty leaves all her furniture and property in the apartment, taking only her personal items. Betty has a Judgment against her for $2,500.00 plus court costs and legal fees. Marla Maples, Manager, posts a Notice of Abandonment, sends a copy certified mail and stores Betty's property for two months. During this time, Betty calls on a couple of occasions and says she will be over to pick up her things but refuses to give a telephone number or address. Betty never comes to the apartment to recover her property (whose value is over $6,000.00) at the end of twenty-one days. Marla Maples, Manager contracts with Modest Moving Company to move, store and sell at public auction Betty's property. Betty then calls and demands her things. Modest Moving quotes Betty and Maples a charge of $1,200.00 to pack and move the property and $50.00 per day to store it, in addition to $500.00 to advertise and set-up the auction. Betty has her lawyer Mel Practice demand in writing, prior to the sale, the return of Betty's property and a reasonable storage charge for Betty to pay. By this time, Betty's bill with Modest is over $1,800.00. The day before the auction, Betty files bankruptcy and the auction is automatically stopped under the federal bankruptcy laws. Modest now presents its bill to Maples Manager for all its costs exceeding $2,500.00. Betty discharges her debt to Maples Manager through her bankruptcy and gets most of her property returned as it is exempt under law and can't be sold to pay her debts. Maples Manager and Modest now must either negotiate a price for Modest's services or sue each other and have a court determine what compensation Modest is entitled to.

Remedy After Termination – *Page 14*

Larry, Moe and Curly Scrouge rent an apartment at Perfect Place Apartments. The three Scrouges become delinquent in their rent and are given a 5-day Notice from manager, Mae Pest, advising them "to pay all rent due within 5-days or their rental agreement will terminate of the 6th day and they must vacate". On the 6th day, the Scrouges move, Mae Pest sues for the remaining months on the Scrouges' lease and the case is heard by a panel of Judges, Chico, Harpo and Groucho Sparks. The Scrouges say they owe nothing after the 6th because they did as they were told (they moved). Judge Harpo is speechless at this defense. Judge Groucho, who rules in favor of Mae Pest, sums up the opinion of the court when he says "You bet your life you owe for the rest of the lease".

Access – *Page 14*

Four brothers rent an apartment at the Abby Lane Complex. The brothers, Paul, John, George and Ringo Bug, are known around the complex as the "Fab Four Party Animals". Manager Mick Stones is concerned about rumors of the "Fab Four" using the carpets in their apartment as an ash tray and delivers a two day access notice to inspect their unit pursuant to A.R.S. Section 33-1343. When Mick tries to enter, he finds the locks have been changed and the tenants refuse to let him enter. Mick then serves a notice terminating the lease immediately and files a forcible detainer complaint for possession of the apartment for damages. At the Court hearing, Judge Yoyo Oh No orders the Fab Four evicted and enters as injunction prohibiting the tenants from refusing access to management to their apartment. Mick Stones inspects the apartment and discovers multiple burns in the apartment's entire carpet. The replacement cost is $2,5000.00. Judge Yoyo Oh No enters Judgment in that amount against the Fab Four and tells them to never make an ash out of themselves again.

Tenant Remedies – *Page 20*

Four roommates, Eddie A. Mean, Huddum Insane, Yessir Airfat and I. A. Tolla, rent an apartment at the Mid East Apartments. All utilities are provided as part of their rental agreement. During a summer storm, lightening strikes the apartment complex and not only knocks out the central air conditioning unit, but causes a fire to start in the residents' apartment. The fire is quickly put out causing only minor smoke damage. In order to repair the air conditioning, Mustard Gas Management must order parts that in turn must be shipped in from out of state. The apartment is without air conditioning for five days. The residents only verbally complain daily until the repairs are finished and then refuse to pay their next month's rent. After a proper 5-day Non-payment Notice and filing of a forcible detainer, the case comes before the Honorable Judge Q. Wait. Judge Wait rules the residents guilty for failure to follow any of the appropriate sections of the Landlord and Tenant Act because the owner took reasonable steps to repair and because the lightening was an "Act of God" over which the owner had no control.

Landlord Noncompliance – *Page 20*

Darrell Queen and Hagan Doss rent an apartment at the Super Sunday Apartments. Manager Millie Vanilli has only one apartment left which is by an area where the grounds are being dug up. That night, manager, Millie Vanilli, sends her leasing hostess, Bea Nana Split, to make sure the barricades are up and the flashing warning lights on. Darrell Queen and Hagan Doss have too much to drink and while walking to their apartment, trip over the barricade, each catching their foot in a rut and each suffers a broken foot. Queen and Doss sue and lose because they cannot show negligence on the part of their apartment complex.

Notice – *Page 27*

Manager I. M. Flakey gave his two most troublesome tenants, Bull Dozier and Jack Hammer, a 30-day Notice that the rental agreement with the Radical Dude Apartment Complex will not be renewed. I. M. Flakey then pre-leases the apartment, effective 5 days after Bull and Jack are to be vacated, to the Bill brothers—Otto and Mo Bill. Bull Dozier and Jack Hammer refuse to move at the end of the 30 days, so on the 31st day, I. M. Flakey files a forcible detainer action to remove them. When Otto and Mo Bill find out they can't move in on the 5th, they are forced to put their property in storage, move to a hotel, and they bring forcible detainer actions against the apartment complex and Bull Dozier and Jack Hammer. When the smoke clears, Judge I. Ain't Lyon awards the complex two month's rent as damages and awards the Bill brothers their out of pocket expenses against both the complex and Jack Hammer and Bull Dozier.

Retaliatory Eviction – *Page 29*

Two sets of tenants rent apartments at the Speak Easy Apartment complex as month-to-month tenants. The Corleone family (Sonny, Michael, Fredo and their godfather, Vito) move into an apartment next to three roommates (Al Carphone, Elliott Mess and Dick Spacey). The Speak Easy Apartment complex develops plumbing problems which both sets of residents complain to the manager, Tex A. Coc and his wife R. Coe about. The Corleone family complains verbally and refuses to pay their rent next month. The Corleones believe this proposed resolution of the plumbing problem is an offer the manager cannot refuse. Tenants Carphone, Spacey and Mess complain in writing on three occasions. Managers Tex A. Coe and R. Coe give both tenants 30-day Notices that they are not renewing both resident leases. Tex A Coe tells R. Coe "This management business is a gas and we'll get these complainers". The next month, the Corleones refuse to pay the rent and move, the manager refuses to take the rent of Carphone and his gang because they have said they won't move and have deducted the cost of the plumbing repairs under A.R.S. Section 33-1363 (self help). Both sets of residents receive Forcible Detainer summons to appear in court. At trial, Judge J. Egghead Hoover orders the Corleone family evicted because their refusal to pay rent allows the manager to legally file a forcible detainer under A.R.S. Section 33-1381(C).

Special Detainers – *Page 34*

Peter Panhandle, a month-to-month tenant, is brought to court for holding over and not moving at the end of a properly given 30-day Notice. Peter calls the court to advise them he has had car trouble and will be late. The case is set for 4:00 P.M. and Never, Never Land Apartments appears on time with their manager, Wendy Wonder, and their attorney Nana Bernard. The court, the Honorable C. Hook presiding, waits until 5:00 P.M. when Peter finally flies in the door. Judge Hook courteously explains the law to Peter and why he has to move, while Peter continually interrupts the Judge and tells Judge Hook he is biased, unfair and hasn't had an original thought since he's been on the bench. Judge Hook tells Peter he does not have to agree with his order, but he does have to follow his order as he says: "There is the door, use it!".

Going to Court – *Page 39*

Ronald and Nancy Raygun, tenants at the White House Apartments, give their proper 30-day Notice that they are moving. Manager Squirrely Temple then re-rents their apartment to Oliver Northwest, who informs Squirrely he will be ready to move in the day after the Rayguns vacate. Ronald Raygun encounters some financial problems and cannot qualify to buy his home and notifies management he will not be moving. Squirrely must put Oliver Northwest up in a motel at her expense until she can evict the Rayguns, because she has no more vacancies. At the eviction hearing, Squirrely asks the court for damages from the Rayguns in an amount of two months' rent or her actual out-of-pocket expense and damages, whichever is greater under A.R.S. Section 33-1375(C). Judge George Bushleague grants Squirrely her damages and orders the Rayguns to move out of the White House in five judicial days.

Trial and Procedure – *Page 39*

Santee Klauss and his son Rudolph rent an apartment at Northern Lights Apartments. Santee is assigned a specific parking space as part of his lease agreement but the lease makes no reference to towing policies. Northern Lights Apartments has no towing signs posted, nor do they record information in their files concerning resident vehicles. Santee Klauss comes home late one night and inadvertently parks in another resident's space. Resident I. M. Phisstoff complains to manager Error N. Progress that someone is in his space. Error, without either posting a towing notice on the vehicle or investigating the situation, calls Miss Steaks 24 Hours Café, Truck Stop and Towing Extravaganza and tows the vehicle. In the process of towing the vehicle, Urkel Jerkle, towing driver, damages Santee's transmission. Santee sues both Northern Lights Apartments and Miss Steaks Towing and wins over the objections of Northern Lights' attorney, Mel Practice.

Going to Court – *Page 39*

Saddam Insane and his wife, Ima Insane, occupy an apartment at the White Flags R US Apartments. Saddam is called into military service and while overseas fails to send the rent money to his wife, instead spending it at the Bunker Tavern. Kitty Litter, manager, serves a 5-day Non-pay Notice to Ima Insane and beings eviction proceedings. Ima Insane asks the court to stay the proceedings because of her husband's military service. Judge O. D. Payne rules that Saddam Insane's presence in not crucial to defend the eviction action and grants the Judgement for possession and rent. However any action to collect on the rent Judgment will be stayed until after Saddam's return.

Judgment – *Page 40*

Two residents, Lennie and Laura Lyar, are evicted from Honest Johns Apartment complex for non-payment of rent. The Lyars refuse to move voluntarily and are forcibly removed by Constable Marvin Mistake. Constable Mistake lets manager, Eleanor Error, have her maintenance people move the Lyars' few personal items to a vacant apartment for storage. No itemization of the property is done. After a couple of weeks, manager Error throws out the property so the apartment be rented. Two months later, the Lyars return and request their property and present a list valued at $7,500.00. The Lyars sue both the apartment complex and the county because a county officer authorized the removal and storage of their property. The Lyars win in Court, and the county must pay for damages.

Appeal – *Page 40*

Ryan Sandwich, Wade Clogs, Trickey Henderson and Darryl Raspberry rent an apartment at the Ball Park Apartments. Trickey Henderson gets hurt one night trying to steal pool furniture that the previous owner of the apartment complex, George Hindender, had rigged to create a dangerous condition for thieves. Red Rose, the current owner of the Ball Park Apartments, found the condition too taxing to correct and left it unchanged. The tenants fail to pay their rent and countersue both Red and George at their eviction hearing for Trickey's injury. The tenants lose, cannot post an appeal bond set by the Judge and are forced to move.

Mobile Home Park
Landlord and Tenant Section

Introduction

During the 1970's the purchase of mobile homes increased dramatically. Americans were looking for a less expensive way to buy a comfortable home and at the same time have the flexibility to move their home without the time and cost associated with selling a residence. As a result more and more mobile home parks were created and laws were enacted to protect the rights of both the landlord and the tenant.

Legislative intent

The legislature recognizes that the legal relationship between the owner of a mobile home, as defined in this act, and the owner of a space which is rented to the owner of the mobile home, is unique in terms of property rights and management. Accordingly, this act should not be construed or interpreted as creating state policy or legislative intent with respect to any property rights, landlord and tenant situation or legal relationships other than the property rights, landlord and tenant situations or legal relationships arising out of rental of mobile home space for a residential mobile home. The legislature intends that this act does not apply to the combined rental of a mobile home space and a mobile home or to recreational vehicles or travel trailers. This act applies when mobile homes are placed on rented spaces.

Exclusions from application of chapter
(A.R.S. Section 33-1407)

   a.   The provisions of this chapter shall not be applicable to an occupancy in or operation of public housing as authorized, provided or conducted under or pursuant to any federal law or regulation which might conflict therewith.

   b.   This chapter is not applicable to a mobile home and mobile home space if both are owned by the same person or to recreational vehicles or travel trailers.

Mobile Home Rental Agreement

Terms and Conditions of Rental Agreement
(A.R.S. Section 33-1413)

   a.   At the beginning of the tenancy, a signed, written rental agreement must be executed by the Landlord or designated agent and tenant. The rental agreement shall be executed in good faith by both parties and shall not provide for the waiver of any rights given to either party by other provisions of this chapter. The rental agreement shall be for a specific period and shall include:

      1.   The amount of the current rent.
      2.   The amount of any security deposit.

   b.   If the landlord and tenant agree to the term of the rental agreements, the rental agreement may be for any term. If the landlord and tenant disagree on the term of the rental agreement, the rental agreement shall be for twelve months. The initial term of a rental agreement may be for less than twelve months if the reason is to ensure conformity with a standard anniversary date. Any written rental agreement shall have all blank spaces completed and executed copies of the written rental agreement shall be furnished to all parties within ten days of execution.

c. The rental agreement may include conditions not prohibited by this chapter or other rule of law governing the rights and obligations of the parties.

d. The landlord shall attach to the rental agreement a statement signed by the prospective tenant acknowledging receipt of:

1. The disclosure required in Section 33-1432.
2. A current copy of this chapter as prescribed in Section 33-1342.
3. A current copy of the rules or regulations adopted pursuant to Section 33-1452.

e. Rent shall be payable without demand or notice at the time and place agreed upon by both the parties. Periodic rent is payable at the beginning of any term of one month or less, and thereafter, unless otherwise agreed, in equal monthly installments at the beginning of each month. Unless otherwise agreed, rent shall be uniformly apportionable from day to day.

f. A landlord shall not prohibit a tenant who is a member of the armed forces of the United States from terminating a rental agreement with less than two weeks' notice to his landlord if he receives reassignment orders which do not allow such prior notification.

g. Notwithstanding any provision of this article to the contrary, upon the expiration or renewal of any rental agreement, the landlord may increase or decrease the total rent or change payment arrangements. The landlord shall notify the tenant in writing by first class or certified mail or by personal delivery at least ninety days prior to the expiration or renewal of any rental agreement of any such increase or change. Nothing in this subsection requires a landlord to provide cause for any change in rent if the landlord complies with notice requirements.

h. On expiration of a written rental agreement for a specified term or written renewal of a rental agreement, tenancy is on a month-to-month basis unless the landlord, its designated agent or the tenant requests a new written rental agreement. If the landlord and tenant agree to the term of the rental agreement, the rental agreement may be for any term. If the landlord and tenant disagree on the term of the rental agreement, the rental agreement shall be for twelve months.

i.   In addition to any other rental provisions, the landlord is entitled to a rental increase effective at the expiration or renewal of any rental agreement or effective immediately if so provided in a written rental agreement to compensate him for actual costs of insurance, taxes and rate increases for utilities, which shall be substantiated by the landlord in writing to the tenant.

j.   As a condition of tenancy the rental agreement may require the prospective tenant to make improvements to the mobile home, including all appurtenances owed by the tenant, to preserve or upgrade the quality of the mobile home park even if the prospective tenant is purchasing a home already located in the mobile home park. The improvement shall not exceed the requirements of the rules or regulations of the mobile home park.

Utility charges *(A.R.S. Section 33-1413.01)*

a.   If a landlord charges separately for gas, water or electricity there shall be a separate meter for every user. For each billing period the cost of the charges for the period shall be separately stated, along with the opening and closing meter readings and the dates of the meter readings. Each bill shall show the computation of the charge generally in accordance with the serving utility company billing format for individual service supplied through a single service meter.

b.   If the landlord separately charges for utilities, the landlord shall not charge more than the prevailing basic service single family residential rate charged by the serving utility or transporter.

Guest fee *(A.R.S. Section 33-1413.02)*

The rental agreement may provide that the landlord may charge a guest fee.

Prohibited Provisions in Rental Agreements; Late Payment Penalty *(A.R.S. Section 33-1414)*

a.   A rental agreement shall not provide that the tenant agrees to:
   1.   Waive or to forego rights or remedies under this chapter.
   2.   Pay the landlord's attorney's fees, except an agreement in writing may provide that attorney's fees may be awarded to the prevailing party in the event of court action.
   3.   The exculpation of limitation of any liability of the landlord arising under law or to indemnify the landlord for that

liability or the costs connected therewith.

4. Permit the landlord to charge a penalty fee for late payment of rent unless a tenant is allowed a minimum of five days beyond the date the rent is due in which to remit payment.

5. Permit the landlord to charge a fee for a guest who does not stay for more than a total of seven days in any calendar month.

b. A provision prohibited by subsection A included in a rental agreement is unenforceable. If a landlord deliberately uses a rental agreement containing a provision known to be prohibited, the tenant may recover actual damages sustained and the rental agreement is voidable by the tenant.

c. A landlord may charge a penalty fee of not to exceed five dollars per day from the due date of the rent for late payment of rent if the payment is not remitted by the sixth day from the due date.

Separation of Rents and Obligation to Maintain Property Forbidden *(A.R.S. Section 33-1415)*

A rental agreement, assignment, conveyance, trust deed or security instrument may not permit the receipt of rent, unless the landlord has agreed to comply with A.R.S. Section 33-1434, subsection A *(see Landlord's Legal Obligations)*.

Regulation of Rents; Preemption by State; Exception *(A.R.S. Section 33-1416)*

a. Notwithstanding any other provision of law, the power to control rents on mobile home spaces is preempted by the state. Cities, including charter cities, or towns do not have the power to control rents.

b. An exception is that subsection A does not apply to mobile home spaces which are owned, financed, insured or subsidized by any state agency, or by any city, including a charter city or town.

Landlord's Obligations

Security Deposits *(A.R.S. Section 33-1431)*

a.   A landlord cannot demand or receive as security however denominated, including but not limited to, prepaid rent in an amount or value in excess of two months' rent.

b.   The landlord must pay not less than five percent annual on any damage, security, cleaning or landscaping deposit received from a tenant. The landlord shall either pay the interest annually or compound the interest annually.

c.   Upon termination of the tenancy, any security deposits shall be returned to the tenant within 14 business days. The security deposit may be applied to the payment of accrued rent and the amount of damages which the landlord has suffered by reason of the tenant's noncompliance of A.R.S. Section 33-1451 *(see Tenant's Obligations)*, if it is itemized by the landlord in a written notice delivered to the tenant together with the amount due within fourteen days of termination of the tenancy and delivery of possession by the tenant. Unlike the Residential Landlord and Tenant Act, no demand need be made by the tenant So it is very important the deposit or itemized statement be sent within the 14-day time period. It is also recommended the tenant always give the landlord a forwarding address.

d.   If the landlord fails to comply, the tenant may recover the property and money due the tenant together with damages in an amount equal to twice the amount wrongfully withheld.

e.   The holder of the landlord's interest in the premises at the time of termination of the tenancy is bound by this section. If the landlord has sold the property, the new owner-landlord is required to comply with this section of the M.H.A.

f.   The amount of any security deposit shall not be changed after the tenant executes the initial rental agreement.

Disclosure and Tender of Written Rental Agreement *(A.R.S. Section 33-1432)*

a.   The landlord or any person authorized to enter into a rental agreement on his behalf shall disclose to the tenant in writing before entering into the rental agreement the name and address of each of the following:

1. The person authorized to manager the premises.
2. The owner of the premises or a person authorized to act for and on behalf of the owner for the purpose of service of process and for the purpose of receiving and receipting for notice and demands.

b. This information must be kept current and furnished to the tenant upon tenant's request. When there is a new owner or operator, this section extends to and is enforceable against any successor landlord, owner or manager.

c. A person who fails to comply becomes an agent of each person who is a landlord for the following purpose:

1. Service of process of lawsuits and receiving and receipting for notices and demands.
2. Performing the obligations of the landlord under the M.H.A. and under the rental agreement and expending or making available for the purpose all rent collected from the premises.

d. The landlord must tender and deliver a signed copy of the rental agreement and a copy of the statement acknowledging receipt to the tenant and the tenant must sign and deliver to the landlord one fully executed copy of such rental agreement and the statement acknowledging receipt within ten days after the agreement is executed if tenant is in possession of the mobile home space or prior to moving onto the mobile home space if he is not in possession of the mobile home space at the time the rental agreement is executed. Such rental agreement shall have all blank spaces completed. The landlord shall deliver to the tenant a signed copy of the rental agreement within ten days after the rental agreement is delivered by the tenant. Noncompliance with this subsection shall be deemed a material noncompliance by the landlord or the tenant, as the case may be, of the rental agreement.

e. The landlord or any person authorized to enter into a rental agreement on his behalf shall post in a conspicuous place a copy of the current utility rates, unless the tenant is charged directly by the utility company.

f. Each tenant shall be notified, in writing, of any rent increase at least sixty days prior to the increase.

g. Before entering into a rental agreement, the landlord or any person authorized to enter into the rental agreement shall proved to the prospective tenant the current Arizona Mobile Home Parks Residential Landlord and Tenant Act booklet, published by the Secretary of State. The landlord shall provide the booklet to the tenant at no cost to the tenant. This subsection shall not apply to the renewal of rental agreements.

h. The landlord shall make available to all tenants revisions to the Arizona Mobile Home Parks Residential Landlord and Tenant Act booklet within sixty days after it is published by the Secretary of State. The landlord shall provide the revisions at no cost to the tenants.

Landlord to Supply Possession of Mobile Home Space
(A.R.S. Section 33-1433)

At the commencement of the term of the rental agreement, the landlord shall deliver possession of the premises to the tenant in compliance with the rental agreement and A.R.S. Section 33-1434 *(see Landlord's Obligations)*. The landlord may bring an action for possession against any person wrongfully in possession and may recover the damages provided in A.R.S. Section 33-1468.

Landlord to Maintain Fit Premises *(A.R.S. Section 33-1434)*

a.   The landlord must:
1. Comply with the requirements of all applicable city, county and state codes materially affecting health and safety of the mobile home park.
2. Make all repairs and do whatever is necessary to put and keep the premises in a fit and habitable condition.
3. Keep all common areas of the premises in a clean and safe condition.
4. Maintain in good and safe working order and condition all swimming pool, shower, bathhouse, electrical, plumbing and sanitary facilities, including recreations halls or meeting facilities supplied or required to be supplied by him.
5. Provide for removal of garbage, rubbish, and other waste incidental to the occupancy of the mobile home park.
6. Furnish outlets for electric, water and sewer services. The landlord shall also furnish a prospective tenant with information concerning the type, size and power rating of all electrical, water and sewer conditions.

b.   A mobile home park landlord shall not impose any conditions of rental or occupancy which restrict the mobile home owner in his choice of a seller of fuel, furnishings, goods, services, or mobile homes connected with the rental or occupancy of a mobile home space unless such condition is necessary to protect the health, safety, aesthetic value, or welfare of mobile home residents in the park. However, the landlord may impose reasonable conditions relating to central gas oil, electricity or water meter systems in the park.

Limitation of Liability *(A.R.S. Section 33-1435)*

a.   Unless otherwise agreed, a landlord who conveys premises that include a mobile home space subject to rental agreement in a good faith sale to a bona fide purchaser is relieved of liability under the rental agreement and the M.H.A. as to events occurring subsequent to written notice to the tenant of the conveyance. He remains liable to the tenant for any right of possession, property, and money to which the tenant is entitled under A.R.S. Section 33-1431 *(see Security Deposits, Mobile Homes)*.

b.   Unless otherwise agreed, a manager of premises that include a mobile home space is relieved of liability under the rental agreement and the M.H.A. as to events occurring after written notice to the tenant of the termination of his management, except such notice shall not terminate any agreement or legal liability.

Statement of Policy; Amendment; Contents; New Statements *(A.R.S. Section 33-1436)*

a.   Before execution of the rental agreement the landlord or any person authorized to enter into the rental agreement shall provide the tenant with the statements of policy of the mobile home park and the date of expiration of each statement. The landlord or any successor in interest shall not delete or amend any statement of policy while it is in force.

b.   The statements of policy shall be attached to the rental agreement and shall include a statement of the following:

1.   The classification of the mobile home park as an adult, family, retirement or mixed use park and any age restrictions for tenants or residents.
2.   The period of time before any change in use is expected.
3.   Any method of determining rent changes.
4.   The right of first refusal on the sale of the mobile home park if any is given to the tenants and under what conditions the right may be executed.
5.   The size and other specifications of mobile homes allowed in the mobile home park including whether the mobile home

must be new or used and whether it must be set at ground level or above ground level.

6. The improvements required as a condition of tenancy.

7. That insuring the mobile home is the tenant's responsibility including fire department respond insurance in unincorporated areas.

c.   At least sixty days before the expiration of a statement of policy, the landlord shall notify all of the tenants of any new statement of policy.

Education Requirements for Park Managers
(A.R.S. Section 33-1437)

a.   Beginning on January 1, 2000, within six months after employment as a park manager, a park manager shall complete at least six hours of educational programs and shall complete at least six additional hours of educational programs every two years.

b.   A park manager shall post proof of completion and compliance with the educational program requirements prescribed by this section in a conspicuous place at the mobile home park.

Tenant's Obligations

Tenant to Maintain Mobile Home Space; Notice of Vacating; Moving Company Notice to Landlord *(A.R.S. Section 33-1451)*

a.   A tenant of a mobile home space shall exercise diligence to maintain that part of the premises which he has rented in as good condition as when he took possession and shall:

1. Comply with all obligations primarily imposed upon tenants by applicable provision of city, county and state codes materially affecting health and safety.

2. Keep that part of the premises that he occupies and uses as clean and safe as the condition of the premises permit.

3. Dispose from his mobile home all rubbish, garbage and other waste in a clean and safe manner as prescribed by park rules.

4. Not deliberately or negligently destroy, deface damage, impair or remove any part of the premises or knowingly permit any person to do so.

5. Conduct himself and require other persons on the premises with his consent to conduct themselves in a manner that will not disturb his neighbors' peaceful enjoyment of the premises.

6. Inform the landlord or manager of the mobile home park at least thirty days before the expiration of the rental agreement that he will not be renewed by the tenant and that the premises will be vacated. If timely notice is not given prior to moving from the mobile home space, the tenant then is responsible for rent equal to an amount consistent with the applicable notice period.

b. The moving company shall report to the landlord or manager of the mobile home park prior to the time a mobile home is being moved in or out of the park.

Rules and Regulations *(A.R.S. Section 33-1452)*

a. A landlord must adopt written rules or regulations, however described, concerning the tenant's use and occupancy of the premises. Such rules or regulations are enforceable against the tenant only if:

1. Their purpose is to promote the convenience, safety or welfare of the tenants on the premises, preserve the landlord's property from abusive use, preserve or upgrade the quality of the mobile home park, or make a fair distribution of services and facilities held out for the tenants generally.
2. They are reasonably related to the purpose for which adopted.
3. They apply to all tenants on the premises in a fair manner.
4. They are sufficiently explicit in prohibition, direction or limitation of the tenant's conduct to fairly inform the tenant of what must or must not be done to comply.
5. They are not for the purpose of evading the obligations of the landlord.
6. The prospective tenant has a copy of the current rules and regulations before he enters into the rental agreement.

b. A new tenant who brings a mobile home into a mobile home park or who purchases an existing mobile home in a mobile home park shall comply with all current rules or regulations.

c. If any mobile home park owner adds, changes, deletes, or amends any rule, a copy of all such additions, changes, deletions or amendments shall be furnished to all mobile home tenants thirty days before they become effective. Any rule or condition of occupancy which is unfair and deceptive or which does not conform to the requirements of this chapter shall be unenforceable. A rule or regulation adopted after the tenant enters into the rental agreement is enforceable against the tenant only if it does not work a substantial modification of the rental agreement.

   d. A person who owns or operates a mobile home park shall not:

      1. Deny rental unless the mobile home is not compatible with the other mobile homes in the park or does not meet the requirements of the statements of policy prescribed pursuant to Section 33-1436 or the park resident or prospective resident cannot conform to park rules and regulations.

      2. Require any person as a precondition to renting, leasing or otherwise occupying a space for a mobile home in a mobile home park to pay an entrance or exit fee of any kind unless for services actually rendered or pursuant to a written agreement.

      3. Deny any resident of a mobile home park the right to sell his mobile home at a price of his own choosing during the term of the tenant's rental agreement, but the landlord may reserve the right to approve the purchaser of such mobile home as a tenant but such permission may not be unreasonably withheld, except that the landlord may require, in order to preserve or upgrade the quality of his mobile home park, that any mobile home not compatible with the other mobile homes in the park or in a rundown condition or in disrepair be removed from the park within sixty days.

      4. Exact a commission or fee with respect to the price realized by the tenant selling his mobile home, unless the park owner or operator has acted as agent for the mobile home owner pursuant to a written agreement.

      5. Require a tenant to use any specific sales agency, manufacturer, retailer or broker.

      6. Require a tenant to furnish permanent improvements which cannot be removed without damage thereto or to the mobile home space by a tenant at expiration of the rental agreement.

      7. Prohibit a tenant from advertising the sale or exchange of his mobile home including the display of a for sale or open house sign on the dwelling or in the window of the mobile home stating the name, address and telephone number of the owner of the mobile home or his agent. The sign may be no larger than twelve inches wide and eighteen inches long. In addition to the display of a sign in the window, the tenants may display the signs on a central posting board in the park which is reasonably accessible to the public seven days a week during daylight hours.

e. The landlord or manager of a mobile home park shall include, in rules and regulations, an emergency number to be called when the park is left unattended, regardless of the size of the park.

f. The landlord shall not prohibit meetings between tenants and invited visiting speakers in the mobile home park relating to mobile home living and affairs in the park community or recreational hall if such meetings are held at reasonable hours and when the facility is not otherwise in use.

g. Any improvements made by a tenant such as plants, vines, edgings, gravel, stone, or other additions made for the benefit of his tenancy may be removed by the tenant, or by agreement of both parties; the landlord may retain the improvements by paying the tenant for their actual costs.

h. If a tenant dies, any surviving joint or co-tenant continue as tenant with the same rights, privileges, and liability as if the surviving tenant were the original tenant, with the additional right to terminate the rental agreement by giving sixty days' written notice to the landlord.

i. If a tenant who was sole owner of the mobile home dies during the term of the rental agreement, the tenant's heirs or legal representative have the right to cancel the lease by giving thirty days' written notice to the landlord with the same rights, privileges, and liabilities of the original tenant.

Access *(A.R.S. Section 33-1453)*

a. The landlord has no right of access to a mobile home owned by a tenant.

b. The landlord and tenant may mutually agree, in writing, to give the landlord access.

Tenant to Use and Occupy as a dwelling Unit; Right to Sublet Mobile Home
(A.R.S. Section 33-1454)

Unless otherwise agreed, the tenant shall occupy his mobile home only as a dwelling unit and may only sublet upon written agreement with the park management.

Landlord's Rights and Remedies

Termination or Nonrenewal of Rental Agreement by Landlord; Noncompliance with Rental Agreement by Tenant; Failure to Pay Rent *(A.R.S. Section 33-1476)*

   a.   The landlord of a mobile home park shall specify the reason or reasons for the termination or nonrenewal of any tenancy in the mobile home park. The reason or reasons relied on for the termination or nonrenewal must be stated in writing with specific facts, so that the date, place and circumstances concerning the reason or reasons for termination or nonrenewal can be determined. Reference to or recital of the language of this chapter, or both, is not sufficient compliance with this subsection.

   b.   The landlord may not terminate or refuse to renew a tenancy without good cause. "Good cause" means:

   1.   Noncompliance with any provision of the rental agreement.
   2.   Nonpayment of rent.
   3.   Change in use of land.
   4.   Clear and convincing evidence that a tenant has repeatedly violated any provision of this chapter and established a pattern of noncompliance with such provisions.

   c.   The landlord's right to terminate or to refuse to renew a tenancy pursuant to subsection B of this section does not arise until the landlord has complied with subsections D, E, or H of this section.

   d.   Except as otherwise prohibited by law:

   1.   If there is a material noncompliance by the tenant with the rental agreement, the landlord must deliver a written notice to the tenant specifying the acts and omissions constituting the breach and that the rental agreement will terminate upon a date not less than thirty days after receipt of the notice if the breach is not remedied in fourteen days.
   2.   If there is a noncompliance by the tenant with Section 33-1451 materially affecting health and safety, the landlord may deliver a written notice to the tenant specifying the acts and omissions constituting the breach and that the rental agreement will terminate upon a date not less than twenty days after receipt of the notice if the breach is not remedied in ten days. However, if the breach is remediable by repair or the payment of damages or otherwise, and the tenant adequately

remedies the breach prior to the date specified in the notice, the rental agreement will not terminate.

3. If there is a noncompliance that is both material and irreparable, and occurs on the premises including an illegal discharge of a weapon, homicide as prescribed in sections 13-1102 through 13-1105, criminal street gang activity as prescribed in section 13-105, activity as prohibited in section 13-2308, prostitution as defined in section 13-3211, the unlawful manufacturing, selling, transferring, possessing, using or storing of a controlled substance as defined in section 13-3451, threatening or intimidating as prohibited in section 13-1202, infliction of serious bodily harm, assault as prohibited in section 13-1203, criminal activity involving serious property damage or acts that have been found to constitute a nuisance pursuant to section 12-991, the landlord may deliver a written notice for immediate termination of the rental agreement and proceed pursuant to section 33-1485.

    If there is a noncompliance which is both material and irreparable and that occurs on the premises, including an unlawful discharge of a weapon, prostitution as defined in section 13-3211, the unlawful manufacture, sale, use, storage, transfer or possession of a controlled substance as defined in section 13-3451, infliction of serious bodily harm, assault as prescribed by section 13-1203 or any other criminal action involving imminent serious property damages, the landlord may deliver a written notice for immediate termination of the rental agreement and proceed pursuant to section 33-1485.

4. If a tenant engages in repetitive conduct that is the subject of notices under this subsection, after two incidents of the same type documented by the landlord within a twelve-month period or after receipt by the landlord of two written complaints from other tenants about the repetitive conduct within a twelve-month period, the landlord may deliver a written notice to the tenant specifying the repetitive conduct and the documentation and advising the tenant that on documentation of the next incident of the same type final notice will be given and the rental agreement or tenancy will be terminated thirty days after the date of the notice.

5. If a tenant has been involved in three or more documented incidents of conduct of any type described in this section within a twelve-month period, the landlord may deliver a written notice to the tenant specifying the conduct and the documentation and advising the tenant that on documentation of the next incident final notice will be given and the rental agreement or tenancy will be terminated thirty days after the date of the notice.

e.   If rent is unpaid when due and the tenant fails to pay rent within seven days after written notice by the landlord of nonpayment an his intention to terminate the rental agreement if the rent is not paid within that period of time, the landlord may terminate the rental agreement. Prior to judgment in an action brought by the landlord under this subsection, the tenant may have the rental agreement reinstated by tendering the past due but unpaid periodic rent, reasonable attorney's fees incurred by the landlord, and court costs, if any.

f.   Except as provided in this chapter, the landlord may recover actual damages, obtain injunctive relief or recover possession of the premises pursuant to an action in forcible detainer for repeated noncompliance by the tenant with the rental agreement or Section 33-1451.

g.   The remedy provided in subsection F of this section is in addition to any right of the landlord arising under subsection D of this section.

h.   If a change in use is intended for the land on which a mobile home park or a portion of a mobile home park is located and the landlord intends eviction of a mobile home tenant due to a change in use, the landlord shall notify all tenants in the park in writing that:

1. The change in use may subsequently result in the termination of a rental agreement.

2. The tenant being terminated due to the change in use will receive a one hundred eighty-day notice before the actual termination of the rental agreement.

Tenant's Rights and Remedies

Noncompliance by the Landlord *(A.R.S. Section 33-1471)*

a.   If there is a material noncompliance by the landlord with the rental agreement, the tenant may deliver a written notice to the landlord specifying the acts and omissions constituting the breach and that the rental agreement will terminate upon a date not less than thirty days after receipt of the notice if the breach is not remedied in fourteen days. If there is a noncompliance by the landlord with A.R.S. Section 33-1434 (*see Landlord's Obligations*), materially affecting health and safety, and omissions constituting the breach and that the rental agreement will terminate upon a date not less than twenty days after receipt of the notice if the breach is not remedied in ten days. The rental agreement shall terminate and the mobile home space shall be vacated as provided in the notice subject to the following:

1. If the breach is remediable by repairs or the payment of damages or otherwise and the landlord adequately remedies the breach prior to the date specified in the notice, the rental agreement will not terminate.

2. The tenant may not terminate for a condition caused by deliberate or negligent act or omission of the tenant, a member of his family, or other person on the premises with his consent.

b.   If a noncompliance by the landlord occurs, the tenant may recover damages, and obtain injunctive relief for any noncompliance by the landlord with the rental agreement or A.R.S. Section 33-1434.

c.   If the rental agreement is terminated, the landlord shall return all deposits less reasonable damages.

Wrongful Failure to Supply Essential Services
(A.R.S. Section 33-1374)

a.   If contrary to the rental agreement or A.R.S. Section 33-1434 (*see Landlord's Obligations*), the landlord deliberately or negligently fails to supply essential services, the tenant may give reasonable notice to the landlord specifying the breach.

b.   The rights under this section do not arise until the tenant has given notice to the landlord. Such rights do not arise if the condition was caused by the deliberate or negligent act or omission of the tenant, a member of his family, or other person on the premises with his consent.

Tenant's Remedies for Landlord's Unlawful Ouster, Exclusion or Diminution of Services *(A.R.S. Section 33-1475)*

If the landlord removes or excludes the tenant from the premises or willfully diminishes services to the tenant by interrupting or causing the interruption of electric, gas, water or other essential service to the tenant, the tenant may recover possession or terminate the rental agreement and, in either case, recover an amount equal to two months' periodic rent and twice the actual damage sustained by him. If the rental agreement is terminated, the landlord shall return all deposits.

If a change is intended in use of land on which a mobile home or a portion of a mobile home is located and the landlord intends eviction of a mobile home tenant due to land use change, the landlord must notify all tenants in the park in writing that:

1. The use of land change may subsequently result in the termination of a rental agreement.
2. The tenant being terminated due to the use of land change will receive a one hundred-eighty days' notice before the actual termination of the rental agreement.

The landlord must provide a one hundred eight days' notice before the actual termination of any rental agreement due to change in use of land.

Change in Use; Notices; Compensation for Moving Expenses; Payments by the Landlord *(A.R.S. Section 33-1476.01)*

a.   The landlord shall notify the director and all tenants in writing of a change in use at least one hundred-eighty days before the change in use. The landlord may not increase rent within ninety days before giving notice of a change of use.

b.   The landlord shall notify all tenants in writing about the mobile home relocation fund established in section 33-1476.02.

c.   If a tenant is required to move due to a change in use, the tenant is entitled to payment from the mobile home relocation fund for the lesser of the actual moving expenses of relocating the mobile home to a new location within a fifty mile radius of the vacated park or an amount of three thousand dollars for a single section mobile home and six thousand dollars for a multisection mobile home. Moving expenses include the cost of taking down, moving and setting up the mobile home in a new location.

d.   Except as provided in subsection F of this section, if there is a change in use the landlord shall pay five hundred dollars for each single section mobile home and eight hundred dollars for each multisection mobile home relocated to the fund for each tenant filing for relocation assistance with the director.

e.   If a change in use occurs before the time stated in the statements of policy and the landlord does not comply with subsection A of this section and with A.R.S. Section 33-1436 and 33-1476, subsection H, the landlord shall pay to the fund in addition to the monies prescribed in subsection D of this section:

1. Five hundred dollars for each mobile home space occupied by a singled section mobile home.
2. Eight hundred dollars for each mobile home space occupied by a multisection mobile home.

f. The landlord is not required to make payments prescribed in subsections D and E of this section for moving mobile homes owned by the landlord or for moving a mobile home under a contract with the tenant if the tenant does not file for relocation assistance with the director.

g. If a change in use occurs within two hundred seventy days of relocations under Section 33-1476.04, the landlord shall pay to the fund in addition to the monies prescribed in subsection D of this section:

1. Five hundred dollars for each mobile home space occupied by a singled section mobile home.
2. Eight hundred dollars for each mobile home space occupied by a multisection mobile home.

h. The tenant shall submit a contract for relocation of a mobile home for approval to the director at least fifteen days before the relocation to be eligible for payment of relocation expenses. The director must approve or disapprove the contract within fifteen days after receipt of the contract, or the contract is deemed to be approved. The payment of expenses shall be made before or at the time of relocation as provided in the rules adopted by the director. If the contract is not approved, the tenant may appeal to the hearing officer.

i. If this state or a political subdivision of this state exercises eminent domain and the mobile home park is sold or a sale is made to this state or political subdivision of this state that intends to exercise eminent domain, the state or political subdivision is responsible for the relocation costs of the tenants.

j. If a tenant is vacating the premises and has informed the landlord or manager before the change in use notice has been given, the tenant is not eligible for compensation under this section.

k. A person who purchases a mobile home already situated in a park or moves a mobile home into a park in which a change in use notice has been given is not eligible for compensation under this section.

l. This section does not apply to a change in use if the landlord moves a tenant to another space in the mobile home park at the landlord's expense.

m. If a tenancy is terminated due to a redevelopment of the mobile home park, the tenant shall have the option of:

> **(a)** Collecting payment from the mobile home relocation fund as described in this section.
>
> **(b)** Abandoning the mobile home in the mobile home park and collecting an amount equal to one-fourth of the maximum allowable moving expenses for the mobile home from the mobile home relocation fund. If the tenant chooses this option, the landlord shall not be required to make the payments prescribed in subsection D. To be eligible, the tenant shall deliver to the landlord the current title to the mobile home duly endorsed by the owner of record and notarized together with valid releases of all liens shown on the title. A copy of those documents shall be delivered to the department in support of the application for payment.

Adopted by Laws 1988, Ch. 208, § 7, effective from and after December 31, 1990. Amended by Laws 1991, Ch. 166, § 10, effective September 21, 1991. Amended by laws 1999, Ch. 277, § 12, effective August 6, 1999.

Mobile Home Relocation Fund; Investment of Monies
(A.R.S. Section 33-1476.02)

a. The mobile home relocation fund is established consisting of monies collected pursuant to A.R.S. Section 33-1476.03.

b. Fund monies shall be used to pay premiums and other costs of purchasing, from a private insurer who is licensed to transact insurance business in this state, insurance coverage for tenant relocation costs due to a change in use as prescribed in A.R.S. Section 33-1476.01. Any insurance rebates shall be deposited in the fund. If such insurance is not available, or if the insurance costs exceed the amount available from the fund, the fund shall be used to make direct payments for tenant relocation costs. Monies in the fund in excess of the amount required for these purposes shall be used, as necessary, to support the hearing officer function under Title 41, Chapter 16, Article 5.

c. The state treasurer shall maintain the fund and shall invest the fund monies. Monies earned on these investments shall be deposited in the fund and shall be used for the same purposes as other fund monies. The state treasurer shall hold at least ten percent of the fund monies for payment of insurance premiums and related costs. Any unexpended and unencumbered monies remaining in the fund at the end of the fiscal year do not revert to the state general fund but remain in the fund, separately accounted for, as a contingency reserve.

d.   The director shall administer the fund and may adopt, amend or repeal rules pursuant to Title 41, Chapter 6 for the administration of the fund. Fund monies shall be paid to the department of building and fire safety to offset the costs of administering the fund. The attorney general shall review the costs charged to the fund.

Assessments for Mobile Home Relocation Fund; Waiver
(A.R.S. Section 33-1476.03)

a.   Beginning with tax year 1989 each owner of a mobile home who has not filed an affidavit of affixture for the mobile home under Section 42-641.01 shall pay each year to the state as assessment equal to a rate of fifty cents per one hundred dollars of the taxable assessed valuation, derived by applying the applicable percentage specified in Section 42-227 to the full cash value, for each mobile home he owns, for the purpose of providing monies for the mobile home relocation fund. The county treasurer shall collect the assessment imposed by this subsection at the same time and in the same manner as unsecured personal property taxes, separately listed on the tax roll, and transfer the revenues collected to the state treasurer for credit to the fund and shall also send to the state treasurer a written notice of the total taxable assessed valuation, derived by applying the applicable percentage specified in Section 42-227 to the full cash value, of all mobile homes in the county on which the assessment prescribed by this section is assessed. The assessment constitutes a lien on the mobile home.

b.   The director shall notify all county assessors to waive the assessment for any year beginning on or after January 1, 1991 if the monies in the fund exceed five million dollars.

c.   If at the end of a fiscal year the amount of monies in the relocation fund is less than three million dollars, the director may reinstate the assessment prescribed by this section.

d.   Except as provided in Subsection F of this section, if there is a change in use the landlord shall pay to the fund:

    1.   The lessor of the actual moving expense of each tenant or two thousand dollars for each single section mobile home and three thousand two hundred dollars for each multisection mobile home relocated between September 1, 1987 and September 1, 1989.

    2.   Five hundred dollars for each single section mobile home and eight hundred dollars for each multisection mobile home relocated from and after September 1, 1989.

e.   If a change in use occurs before the time stated in the statements of policy and the landlord does not comply with Section 33-1436, Section 33-1476. Subsection H, and Section 33-1476.01, Subsection A, the landlord shall pay to the fund in addition to the monies prescribed in Subsection D of this section:

1.   Five hundred dollars for each mobile home space occupied by a single section mobile home.

2.   Eight hundred dollars for each mobile home space occupied by a multisection mobile home.

f.   The landlord is not required to make the payments prescribed in subsection E of this section for moving mobile homes owned by the landlord.

g.   The tenant shall submit a contract for relocation of a mobile home for approval to the director at least sixty days before the relocation to be eligible for payment of relocation expenses. The director shall approve or disapprove the contract within fifteen days after receipt of the contract or the contract is deemed to be approved. The payment of expenses shall be made as provided in the rules adopted by the director. If the contract is not approved, the tenant may appeal to the hearing officer.

h.   If at the end of any fiscal year the amount of monies in the relocation fund is less than three million dollars, the director may reassess the tenants for payment into the fund pursuant to subsection B of this section.

Relocations due to rent increase; mobile home relocation fund; applicability *(A. R. S. Section 33-1476.04)*

a.   A tenant is eligible for payment from the mobile home relocation fund if all of the following conditions are met:

1.   The tenant resides in a mobile home that is owned by the tenant and that is located in a mobile home park.

2.   A rent increase will be effective at the expiration or renewal of the tenant's rental agreement.

3.   The rent increase either singly or in combination during any consecutive twelve month period is more than a total of ten percent plus the current increase in the consumer price index over the most recent one year period before the date of the notice of the rent increase. In this paragraph, "consumer price index" means the "WEST-A" index that is published

by the United States Department of Labor, Bureau of Labor Statistics, and that demonstrates changes in prices in certain cities in the western United States.

b. A landlord who increases rent as prescribed by subsection A of this section shall give written notice of the applicability of this section to all affected tenants.

c. A tenant is eligible to receive relocation expenses pursuant to subsection A of this section as follows.

1. At least thirty days before the effective date of the rent increase that exceeds the limits prescribed by subsection A of this section, the tenant shall submit a contract for relocation of the mobile home to the director for approval and to the landlord.

2. Before the effective date of the rent increase, the tenant shall relocate the mobile home or have a fully signed contract with a licensed moving company to move the mobile home to a specific location by a specific date and must have moved the mobile home pursuant to that contract within forty-five days after the effective date of the rent increase.

3. The director shall approve or disapprove the contract submitted within fifteen days after receipt of the contract, and the contract is deemed to be approved on the sixteenth day if the director takes no action. The payment of relocation expenses shall be made at or before the time of relocation as provided in rules adopted by the director. If the contract is not approved, the tenant may appeal to an administrative law judge pursuant to title 41, chapter 16, article 5. The tenant shall provide notice pursuant to section 33-1451, subsection A, paragraph 6 if the tenant relocates.

4. On approval, the tenant is eligible for the lesser of the actual moving expenses of relocating the mobile home or FIVE thousand dollars for a single section mobile home or TEN thousand dollars for a multisection mobile home. Compensable moving expenses include the cost of taking down, moving and setting up the mobile home in the new location if the mobile home is relocated to a residential location within a one hundred mile radius of the vacated mobile home park.

d. This section does not apply to rent increases that are prescribed in a written rental agreement.

e. Nothing in this section shall be construed to make any rent increase unreasonable.

Failure to Maintain *(A.R.S. Section 33-1477)*

If there is noncompliance by the tenant with A.R.S. Section 33-1351 *(see Tenant's Obligations)* materially affecting health and safety that can be remedied by repair, replacement of a damaged item or cleaning and the tenant fails to comply as promptly as conditions require in case of emergency or within ten days after written notice by the landlord specifying the breach and requesting that the tenant remedy it within that period of time, the landlord may enter the mobile home space, and cause the work to be done in a workmanlike manner and submit an itemized bill for the actual and reasonable cost of the fair and reasonable value thereof additional as rent on the next date when periodic rent is due, or if the rental agreement was terminated, for immediate payment.

Remedies for Abandonment *(A.R.S. Section 33-1478)*

a. If the tenant abandons the mobile home unit on a mobile home space, it is incumbent upon the landlord to locate the legal owner or lienholder of the mobile home unit within ten days and communicate to him his liability for any costs incumbered for the mobile home space for such mobile home unit, including rental and utilities due and owing. However, the landlord is entitled to a maximum of sixty days' rent due prior to notice to lienholder. Any and all costs then become the responsibility of the legal owner or lienholder of the mobile home. The mobile home unit may not be removed from the mobile home space without a signed written agreement from the mobile home park landlord, owner or manager showing clearance for removal, showing all monies due and owing paid in full, or an agreement reached with the legal owner and the landlord.

b. A required standardized registration form shall be filled out by each mobile home space renter, upon mobile space rental, showing mobile home make, year, serial number and license number if any be legally required, and also showing if the mobile home is paid for, if there is a lien on the mobile home, and if so the lienholder, and who is the legal owner of the mobile home unit. The registration must be kept on file with the park management as long as the mobile home is on the mobile home space within the park. Notice shall be given to park management within ten days of any changes in a new lien, changes of existing lien or settlement of lien.

c.   In any contested action arising out of an agreement entered into pursuant to the M.H.A. or for violation of any provisions of the Act, the court may award the successful party reasonable attorney's fees. The award of reasonable attorney's fees should be made to mitigate the burden of the expense of litigation to establish a just claim or a just defense. It need not equal or relate to the attorney's fees actually paid or contracted by such award and may not exceed the amount paid or agreed to be paid. Reasonable attorney's fees shall be awarded by the court upon clear and convincing evidence that the claim or defense constitutes harassment, is groundless and not made in good faith. In making such award, the court may consider such evidence as it deems appropriate and shall receive such evidence during trial on the merits of the case, or separately, regarding the amount of such fees as it deems in the best interest of the parties.

d.   Treble damages may be awarded to either the landlord or the tenant by the court in any contested action arising under this chapter upon clear and convincing evidence that the claim or defense constitutes harassment, is groundless and not made in good faith. Again, the court may consider such evidence as it deems appropriate and shall receive this evidence during the trial on the merits of the case, or separately. If the action is brought in Justice Court and a party intends to request treble damages, the party shall file with the Justice Court a pleading stating that treble damages are sought and that the Justice Court may lawfully award treble damages within the court's jurisdiction of civil actions. In absence of such pleading, the Justice of the Peace may not award treble damages. If an opposing party files a verified pleading alleging that court's jurisdiction of civil actions ($2,499), then the case would be transferred to Superior Court for all further proceedings.

Recovery of Possession Limited *(A.R.S. Section 33-1482)*

A landlord may not recover or take possession of the mobile home space by action or otherwise, including willful diminution of services to the tenant by interrupting or causing the interruption of electric, gas, water, or other essential service to the tenant, except in case of abandonment, surrender or a permitted by the M.H.A.

Periodic Tenancy; Holdover Remedies
(A.R.S. Section 33-1483)

a.   The landlord may terminate a tenancy only as provided under A.R.S. Section 33-1476 above.

b. If the tenant remains in possession without the landlord's consent after expiration of the rental agreement or its termination, the landlord may bring an action for possession and if the tenant's holdover is willful and not in good faith the landlord in addition may recover an amount equal to not more than two months' periodic rent and twice the actual damages sustained by him.

Landlord and Tenant Remedies for Abuse of Access
(A.R.S. Section 33-1484)

a. If the tenant refuses to allow lawful access to his mobile home, the landlord may terminate the rental agreement and may recover actual damages.

b. If the landlord makes an unlawful entry or a lawful entry in an unreasonable manner or makes repeated demands for entry otherwise lawful but which have the effect of unreasonably harassing the tenant, the tenant may obtain injunctive relief to prevent the recurrence of the conduct or terminate the rental agreement. In either case, the tenant may recover actual damages not less than an amount equal to one month's rent plus attorney's fees, plus any unused prepaid rent.

c. The landlord of a mobile home park shall specify the reason for the termination of any tenancy in such mobile home park. The reason relied on for the termination must be set forth with specific facts, so that the date, place and circumstances concerning the reason for termination can be determined. Reference to or recital of the language of the M.H.A., or both, is not sufficient.

d. Notwithstanding subsections A and B above, a landlord may bring an action for eviction if either of the following occurs:

> **1.** The violation of the applicable building or housing code was caused primarily by lack of reasonable care by the tenant or other person in his household or upon the premises with his consent.
>
> **2.** The tenant is in default in rent.

Retaliatory Action

Retaliatory Conduct Prohibited; Eviction
(A.R.S. Section 33-1491)

   a.   Except as provided in this section, a landlord shall not retaliate by increasing rent or decreasing service or by bringing or threatening to bring an action for eviction after any of the following:

1. The tenant has complained to a government agency, charged with responsibility for enforcement of a building or housing code of a violation applicable to the premises materially affecting health and safety.
2. The tenant has complained to the landlord of a violation under this chapter.
3. The tenant has organized or become a member of a tenant's union or similar organization.
4. The tenant has filed an action against the landlord in the appropriate court or with the appropriate hearing officer.

   b.   If the landlord acts in violation of subsection A of this section, the tenant is entitled to the remedies provided in Section 33-1475 and has a defense in action against him for eviction. In an action by or against the tenant, evidence of a complaint within six months prior to the alleged act of retaliation creates a presumption that the landlord's conduct was in retaliation. The presumption does not arise if the tenant made the complaint after notice of termination of the rental agreement. For the purpose of this subsection, "presumption" means that the trier of fact must find the existence of the fact presumed unless and until evidence is introduced which would support a finding of its nonexistence.

   c.   The landlord of a mobile home park shall specify the reason for the termination of any tenancy in such mobile home park. The reason relied on for the termination shall be set forth with specific facts, so that the date, place and circumstances concerning the reason for termination can be determined. Reference to or recital of the language of this chapter, or both, is not sufficient compliance with this subsection.

   d.   Notwithstanding subsections A and B of this section, a landlord may bring an action for eviction if either of the following occurs:

1. The violation of the applicable building or housing code was caused primarily by lack of reasonable care by the tenant or other person in his household or upon the premises with this

consent.

2.   The tenant is in default in rent. The maintenance of the action does not release the landlord from liability under Section 33-1471, subsection B.

Mobile Home Parks Hearing Officer Function

Establishment; Duties *(A.R.S. Section 41-2198)*

A mobile home park's hearing office function is established in the department. The director shall promulgate rules relating to the mobile home park's hearing officer function. The hearing office shall adjudicate complaints regarding and ensure compliance with the Arizona Mobile Home Parks Residential Landlord and Tenant Act and rules promulgated pursuant to this section

Hearing Officer' Rights and Procedures
(A.R.S. Section 41-2198.01)

a.   A person who is subject to Title 33, Chapter 11 of a party to a rental agreement entered into pursuant to Tile 33, Chapter 11 and who has paid the required annual fee may petition the department for a hearing concerning violations of the Arizona Mobile Home Parks Residential Landlord and Tenant Act and rules promulgated pursuant to this article by filing a petition with the department and paying a fifty dollar filing fee. All monies collected shall be deposited in the state general fund and are not refundable.

b.   The petition shall be in writing on a form approved by the department, shall list the complaints and shall be signed by or on behalf of the persons filing and include their address, stating that a hearing is desired, and shall be filed with the department.

c.   On receipt of the petition and the filing fee the department shall mail by certified mail a copy of the petition along with notice to the named respondent that a response is required within ten days of mailing of the petition showing cause, if any, why the petition should be dismissed.

d.   After receiving the response, the director of his designee shall promptly review the petition for hearing and, if justified, refer the petition to the mobile home parks hearing officer who shall set a time and place for a hearing and shall give the parties not fewer than fifteen days notice of the hearing. The director may dismiss a petition for hearing if it appears to his satisfaction that the disputed issue or issues have been resolved by the parties.

e.   Failure of the respondent to answer is deemed an admission of the allegations made in the petition and the hearing officer may proceed with a default hearing.

f.   Informal disposition may be made of any contested case.

g.   Either party to a hearing may present witnesses on his behalf, in person or by deposition, on making a request to the hearing officer and designating the person or persons requested to be subpoenaed and may request that a written transcript of the hearing be taken and made upon payment of the cost of the transcript. For the purpose of the hearing, the hearing office has the powers vested in public officers by Section 12-2212. The hearing officer may cause the deposition of witnesses within or without this state to be taken as prescribed by law for deposition in civil cases.

h.   Either party or his authorized agent may inspect any file of the department that pertains to the hearing, if such authorization is filed in writing with the department.

Hearing Officer; Orders; Penalties; Disposition
(A.R.S. Section 41-2198.02)

a.   After the hearing is concluded the hearing officer shall issue a written order within fifteen days. The hearing officer may order any party to abide by the statute or contract provision at issue and levy an administrative penalty on the basis of each violation. All monies collected pursuant to this article shall be deposited in the state general fund to be used to offset the cost of administering the hearing officer function. If the petitioner prevails, the hearing officer shall order the respondent to pay to the petitioner the filing fee required by Section 41-2198.01.

b.   The order issued by the hearing officer is binding o the parties unless a rehearing is granted pursuant to Section 41-2198.04 based on a petition setting forth the reasons for the request for rehearing, in which case the order issued at the conclusion of the rehearing is binding on the parties. The order issued by the hearing officer is enforceable through contempt of court proceedings.

Scope of Hearing *(A.R.S. Section 41-2198.03)*

The mobile home parks hearing officer may hear and adjudicate all matters relating to the Arizona Mobile Home Parks Residential Landlord and Tenant Act and rules promulgated pursuant to this article, except that the hearing officer shall not hear matters pertaining to rental increases pursuant to Section 33-1413 subsection G or I and does not have the authority to impose civil penalties. This section shall not be construed to limit the jurisdiction of the courts of this state to hear and decide matters pursuant to the Arizona Mobile Home Park Residential Landlord and Tenant Act.

Rehearing; Appeal *(A.R.S. Section 41-2198.04)*

a.   Within twenty days after service of notice of the decision of the hearing officer, a person aggrieved by a decision of the hearing officer may apply for a rehearing by filing with the director a petition in writing. Within ten days after filing such petition, the director shall serve notice of the request on the other party by mailing a copy of the petition in the manner prescribed in Section 41-2198.01 for notice of hearing. The filing of a petition for rehearing shall be a condition precedent to any right of appeal as prescribed pursuant to subsection E of this section.

b.   The filing of a petition for rehearing temporarily suspends the operation of the hearing officer's action. If the petition is granted, the hearing officer's action is suspended pending the decision on the rehearing.

c.   In the order granting or denying a rehearing, the direction shall include a statement of the particular grounds and reasons for the director's action on the petition and shall promptly mail a copy of the order to the parties who have appeared in support of or in opposition to the petition for rehearing. If a rehearing is granted, the hearing officer shall set the matter for further hearing on due notice to the parties, given in the manner prescribed in Section 41-2198.01 for notice of an original hearing. Within ten days after submission of the matter on rehearing, the hearing officer shall render a decision in writing and give notice of the decision the same manner as of a decision rendered on an original hearing.

d.   In a rehearing conducted pursuant to this section, a corporation may be represented by a corporate office or employee who is not a member of the state bar if:

1. The corporation has specifically authorized such officer or employee to represent it.
2. Such representation is not the officer's or employee's primary duty to the corporation but is secondary or incidental to such officer's or employee's duties relating to the management or operation of the corporation.

e.   An action to review a final administrative decision of the director shall be pursuant to Title 12, Chapter 7, Article 6, except that the director shall have thirty days to prepare and file with the court a transcript of the proceedings before the director.

Top 10 Tips –
Landlords and Tenants of Mobile Homes

1. Landlord and tenants (and potential ones) should read the Arizona Landlord and Tenant Act. (Copies are available from the Secretary of State's Office, 1700 West Washington Street) The law details the rules that apply to landlords and tenants.

2. Potential tenants, before signing a lease, should inspect a rental site to ensure everything is in working order and in good condition. Make a list of needed repairs and make sure to get the landlord to sign it. Otherwise, tenants may be charged for those damages when they move out. Ask residents about living conditions and if they have criticisms.

3. Tenants should read a lease carefully before signing it. See what provisions there are for breaking and renewing the lease. Keep a copy of the lease in case questions arise later.

4. Tenants should know which charges, such as security and cleaning deposits, are refundable. Nonrefundable cleaning and redecorating deposits must be stated in writing.

5. Tenants always should pay their rent by check or money order. Get a written receipt. The check or money order stub and receipt serve as verification of payment in case there is any questions in the future.

6. Tenants should make all requests for repairs in writing, keeping their own copies. If they want to do their own repairs or improvements – and be reimbursed – they first should outline the arrangements in writing and get the landlord to sign the paper.

7. Tenants should never withhold rent to force a landlord to make repairs. Check the Landlord and Tenant Act, which specifies what to do regarding the landlord's refusal to make repairs.

8. Tenants and landlords should not enter into verbal agreements. Put all agreement in writing, and keep copies of these agreements. If a problem develops on either side, the documents can be consulted.

9. Landlords should put all notices in writing and deliver them in person or by certified or registered mail. This ensures that the tenant receives them.

10. Landlords should return all refundable security deposits or an itemized list of deductions to tenants within 14 days of the termination of the lease. The money may be applied to rental payments and any damages.

Commercial Leases

The law in Arizona regarding commercial lease is governed by either the lease itself or statute. It is extremely important that both landlord and tenant read and know their lease. Your rights and obligations should be set forth in great detail in the lease. This would include but not be limited to payment or rent, subletting, default and termination of the lease.

In addition a few Arizona statutes do apply to commercial rental arrangements. These are found in A.R.S. Section 33-341 to A.R.S. Section 33-361 and A.R.S. Section 33-1023. The most important sections of the law allow a landlord, at his option, to reenter a tenant's property without notice of any kind, and lock the tenant out of the property if the tenant is delinquent in rent for five days or when a tenant violates any provision of the lease. The landlord can also hold the tenant's property for sixty days and if rent is not paid within that time period can sell the property at public auction and apply the proceeds of the sale to any charges that are due and owing. Notice must be given to the tenant of the proposed sale and an accounting of any sale proceeds receive must be done by the landlord.

Bankruptcy

Both landlords and tenant should be aware of their rights and responsibilities if ever involved in a bankruptcy case. The filing of bankruptcy is governed by federal law and as such, has priority over state law (the Arizona Residential Landlord and Tenant Act). Bankruptcies can either be a complete discharge of debts (Chapter 7) or a reorganization of debts and repayment pursuant to a court order (Chapter 11 or 13).

Once a tenant files a bankruptcy, an automatic stay or restraining order goes into effect against all creditors, including a landlord and no legal action can be taken without approval of the bankruptcy court. The landlord must file a motion to lift the automatic stay before proceeding with an eviction action. The option to lift the automatic stay can take from approximately 30 days to four (4) months to complete depending upon whether the tenant contests it. During this time, the tenant can continue to live in the apartment or rental house. However, the tenant is to keep all rent current from the date they file their bankruptcy.

One exception to the above is that if a landlord has obtained their eviction Judgment or court order before the tenant files bankruptcy, the state court has the option to let the landlord recover physical possession of the rental property, but not collect on the money portion of the Judgment. It is highly recommend when either filing bankruptcy or dealing with someone who has filed, you consult a reputable attorney.

General Provisions

The underlying purposes and policies of Arizona's Mobile Home Act was:

1. To simplify, clarify and establish the law governing the rental of mobile home spaces and rights and obligations of landlord and tenant, and,

2. To encourage landlord and tenant to maintain and improve the quality of mobile home housing.

Jurisdiction and Service of Process; Recovery of Attorney's Fees; Treble Damages *(A.R.S. Section 33-1408)*

a. The appropriate Arizona court, whether it be a Justice Court or Superior Court of the county where the landlord and tenant reside, may exercise jurisdiction over any landlord with respect to any claim arising from a transaction subject to the Mobile Home Act. In addition to any other method provided by court, rule or by statute, personal jurisdiction over a landlord may be acquired in civil action or proceeding instituted in the appropriate court by the service of process in the manner provided by the Mobile Home Act.

b. If a landlord is not a resident of this state or is a corporation not authorized to do business in this state and engages in a transaction subject to the Mobile Home Act, he shall designate an agent upon whom service of process of lawsuits may be made in this state. The agent has to be a resident of Arizona or a corporation authorized to do business in the state. The designation shall be in writing and filed with the Secretary of State. If no designation is made and filed or if process cannot be served in this state upon the designated agent, process may be served upon the Secretary of State, but the plaintiff or petitioner shall forthwith mail a copy of this process and pleading by registered or certified mail to the defendant or respondent at his last reasonable ascertained address. If there is no last reasonably ascertainable address and if the defendant or respondent has not complied with A.R.S. Section 33-1432, subsections A and B, then service upon the Secretary of State shall be sufficient service of process without the mailing of copies to the defendant or respondent. Service of process shall be deemed complete and the time shall begin to run for the purpose of this section at the time of service upon the Secretary of State. The defendant must appear in court and answer within thirty days after service in the manner and under the same penalty as if he had been personally served with the summons. An affidavit of compliance with this section shall be filed with the Clerk of the Court on or before the return day of the process, if any, or within any further time the court allows. Where applicable, the affidavit shall contain a statement that defendant or respondent has not complied with A.R.S. Section 33-1432 *(see Landlord's Legal Obligations)*, subsections A and B or affiant could not ascertain compliance by inquiry directed to the Secretary of Sate. It is always advisable to use your attorney or at least consult with an attorney prior to beginning a lawsuit so that all procedural steps are properly followed.

Residential, Landlord, Tenant

Part 1

General Definitions *(A.R.S. Section 33-1310)*

Subject to additional definitions contained in subsequent articles of this chapter which apply to specific articles thereof, and unless the context otherwise requires in this chapter:

1. "Action" includes recoupment, counterclaim, setoff, suit in equity and any other proceeding in which rights are determined, including an action for possession.

2. "Building and housing codes" include any law, ordinance or governmental regulation concerning fitness for habitation, or the construction, maintenance, operation, occupancy, use or appearance of any premises, or dwelling unit.

3. "Delivery of possession" means returning dwelling unit keys to the landlord and vacating the premises.

4. "Dwelling unit" means a structure or the part of a structure that is used as a home, residence, or sleeping place by one person who maintains a household or by two or more persons who maintain a common household. "Dwelling unit" excludes real property used to accommodate a mobile home, unless the mobile home is rented or leased by the landlord.

5. "Good faith" means honesty in fact in the conduct or transaction concerned.

6. "Landlord" means the owner, lessor or sublessor of the dwelling unit or the building of which it is a part, and it also mans a manager of the premises who fails to disclose as required by Section 33-1322.

7. "Organization" includes a corporation, government, governmental subdivision or agency, business trust, estate, trust, partnership or association, two or more persons having a joint or common interest and any other legal or commercial entity which is a landlord, owner, manager or constructive agent pursuant to Section 33-1322.

8. "Owner" means one or more persons, jointly or severally, in whom is vested all or part of the legal title to property or all or part of the beneficial ownership and a right to present use and enjoyment of the premises. The term includes a mortgagee in possession.

9. "Person" means an individual or organization.

10. "Premises" means a dwelling unit and the structure of which it is a part and existing facilities and appurtenances therein, including furniture and utilities where applicable, and grounds, areas and existing facilities held out for the use of tenants generally or whose use is promised to the tenant.

11. "Rent" means payments to be made to the landlord in full consideration for the rented premises.

12. "Rental agreement" means all agreements, written, oral or implied by law, and valid rules and regulations adopted under Section 33-1342 embodying the terms and conditions concerning the use and occupancy of a dwelling unit and premises.

13. "Roomer" means a person occupying a dwelling unit that lacks a major bathroom or kitchen facility, in a structure where one or more major facilities are used in common by occupants of the dwelling unit and other dwelling units. Major facility in the case of a bathroom means toilet, or either a bath or shower, and in the case of a kitchen means refrigerator, stove or sink.

14. "Security" means money or property given to assure payment or performance under a rental agreement. "Security" does not include a reasonable charge for redecorating or cleaning.

15. "Single family residence" means a structure maintained and used as a single dwelling unit. Notwithstanding that a dwelling unit shares one or more wall with another dwelling unit, it is a single family residence if it has direct access to a street or thoroughfare and shares neither heating facilities, hot water equipment nor any other essential facility or service with any other dwelling unit.

16. "Tenant" means a person entitled under a rental agreement to occupy a dwelling unit to the exclusion of others.

17. "Term of lease" means the initial term or any renewal or extension of the written rental agreement currently in effect not including any wrongful holdover period.

Mobile Home Park, Landlord, Tenant
Part 2

General Definitions *(A.R.S. Section 33-1409)*

1. "Action" includes recoupment, counterclaim, setoff, suit in equity and any other proceeding in which rights are determined, including an action for possession.

2. "Anniversary date" means an annual date applying to all tenants stated in the rental agreement on which the landlord may adjust the amount of rent.

3. "Appurtenances" means awnings, sheds, porches and other attachments to the mobile home.

4. "Building and housing codes" includes any law, ordinance or governmental regulation concerning fitness for habitation, or the construction, maintenance, operation, occupancy, use or appearance of any premises, dwelling unit or mobile home space.

5. "Change in use" means either a change in the use of land from the rental of mobile home spaces in a mobile home park to some other use, or the redevelopment of the mobile home park.

6. "Compatible" means a mobile home which is in a similar condition as the majority of the other mobile homes in the mobile home park, as determined by the maintenance, condition and overall appearance of the mobile home.

7. "Director" means the director of the department of building and fire safety.

8. "Dwelling unit" excludes real property used to accommodate a mobile home.

9. "Educational program" means a class, workshop or educational convention that primarily instructs attendees on issues dealing with the operation of a mobile home park and that is sponsored by a nonprofit organization whose sole or primary purpose is the advocacy and promotion of the rental mobile home parks industry.

10. "Fund" means the mobile home relocation fund.

11. "Good faith" means honesty in fact in the conduct or transaction concerned.

12. "Guest" means a nonresident, over and above the occupancy limit set for the resident's space under the terms of the rental agreement or by park rules, of a mobile home park who stays at the home of a person with constructive possession of the home with the consent of the resident for one or more nights and not more than thirty days in any twelve month period.

13. "Landlord" means the owner, lessor, sublessor or operator, or any combination thereof of a mobile home park and it also means a manager of the premises who fails to disclose as required by § 33-1432.

14. "Mobile home" :

    a. Means either of the following:

        (i) A residential structure manufactured on or before June 15, 1976, that is transportable in one or more sections, eight feet or more in body width over thirty feet in body length with the hitch, built on an integral chassis, designed to be used as a dwelling when connected to the required utilities and not originally sold as a travel trailer or recreational vehicle and which includes the plumbing, heating, air conditioning and electrical systems in the structure.

        (ii) A manufactured home built after June 15, 1976, originally bearing an appropriate insignia of approval issued by the United States Department of Housing and Urban Development.

    b. Does not include either of the following:

        (i) A recreational vehicle such as a motor home, camping trailer, van, fifth wheel trailer or other type of recreational vehicle.

        (ii) A structure known as a park model trailer that is a structure built on a single chassis, mounted on wheels and designed to be connected to the utilities necessary for the operation of installed fixture and appliances and that has a gross interior area of not less than three hundred twenty square feet when prepared for occupancy.

15. "Mobile home park" means any parcel of land that contains four or more mobile home spaces.

16. "Mobile home space" means a parcel of land for rent which has a been designed to accommodate a mobile home and provide the required sewer and utility connections.

17. "Moving expenses" means the cost incurred by the tenant whose mobile home is moved for taking down, transporting and setting up the mobile home with the identical, or substantially similar, improvements as were attached to the tenant's mobile home on the mobile home space from which it was removed but does not include the cost of landscaping of the cost of utility lines, trenching or utility connections located in excess of twenty-five feet from the point of hookup on the mobile home.

18. "Organization" includes a corporation, limited liability company, government, governmental subdivision or agency, business trust, estate, trust, partnership or association, two or more persons having a joint or common interest and any other legal or commercial entity which is a landlord, owner, manager or designated agent pursuant to § 33-1432.

19. "Owner" means one or more persons, jointly or severally, in whom is vested all or part of legal title to property or all or part of the beneficial ownership and a right to present use and enjoyment of the premises. The term includes a mortgagee in possession.

20. "Park manager" means the person who is primarily responsible for the day to day operation of a mobile home park.

21. "Person" includes a company, partnership or firm as well as a natural person.

22. "Premises" means the mobile home park and its existing facilities and appurtenances, including furniture and utilities where applicable, and grounds, areas and existing facilities held out for the use of tenants generally or whose use is promised to the tenant.

23. "Prospective tenant" means a person who desires to become a tenant.

24. "Redevelopment of the mobile home park" means that the spaces being redeveloped shall remain vacant for at least one hundred eighty days after the effective date of all change in use notices that are given to the tenants and:

    (a) A minimum of twenty-five percent of the spaces in the park are being changed into an upgraded mobile home park.

    (b) A minimum of twenty-five of the total number of spaces in the park are being changed into an upgraded mobile home park.

25. "Rent" means payments to be made to the landlord or designated agent in full consideration for the rented premises.

26. "Rental agreement" means leases or agreements and valid rules adopted under § 33-1452 embodying the terms and conditions concerning the use and occupancy of a mobile home space and premises, and includes month-to-month tenancies that arise out of the expiration of a written rental agreement pursuant to § 33-1413.

27. "Resident" means a person entitled under a rental agreement to occupy a mobile home space to the exclusion of others and does not include a person rendering necessary live-in care under § 33-1413.03.

28. "Security" or "security deposit" means any refundable money or property given to assure payment or performance under a rental agreement.

29. "Tenant" means a person signing a rental agreement or otherwise agreeing with a landlord for the occupancy of a mobile home space.

30. "Visitor" means a nonresident of a mobile home park who stays at the home of a resident with the consent of the resident but does not stay overnight.

Slumlord Laws

In August 1999, the Arizona Legislature passed what is commonly called the *"Slumlord Bill"*. This Bill gives the governmental authorities great power over crime and "slum" type properties. The law specifically states the following.

If a residential property is regularly used in the commission of a crime, it may be declared a nuisance. The government may then enjoin, abate or prevent any type of criminal activity. If the Attorney General, County Attorney, City Attorney or resident of the area believes they are affected by a nuisance, they may bring an action in Superior Court against the owner, the management agent or any other party responsible for the property to stop the criminal activity. Any penalties that are assessed, however, must require proof against a person that the person knew or had reason to know of the criminal activity.

The owner is now required to take any reasonable, legally available actions to stop the criminal activity on the premises. If the government files action to come in and stop the nuisance, the court may assess the owner for the cost of abating or stopping the nuisance. Any fine that is assessed is prior to any other liens, obligations, or encumbrances except for prior recorded mortgages and a few other liens. The owner or agent is deemed to know or have reason to know of the nuisance is the owner or owner's agent has received notice of documented reports of criminal offences from a governmental authority occurring on the residential property. This notice can be served in person or by certified mail or even published in the newspaper if the owner or agent cannot be located.

Additionally, the court can enter a temporary restraining order against the owner to prevent or abate a continuance or reoccurrence of the criminal activity. At any hearing, evidence of the general reputation of a property, building or place is admissible for the purpose of proving the existence of the nuisance. In other words, tenants or neighbors could testify that the police are called regularly to the property or it is known as an area of common drug dealing, etc.

As indicated above, in addition to entering a restraining order, the court can order the owner to pay damages. These can include expenses incurred in abating the nuisance, the cost of investigation and enforcement of any restraining order, the costs of compensation for a temporary receiver, if one is appointed, and order a civil penalty of not more than $10,000.00.

If there is a second violation within a three (3) year period of the first, the court may order the property owner to pay three (3) times the cost of the abatement.

If a tenant or neighbor brings an action, and the court finds there was no reasonable basis for that action, the court may assess costs and attorney's fees against the resident. However, if the court finds in favor of the resident, it may award costs and reasonable attorney's fees against the property owner.

Additionally, if you purchase a property that is subject to an abatement action, that does not terminate the action. You are deemed to have Notice of the action. This applies also to any sale or transfer.

Additionally, the courts have the authority to close the property if they find that a nuisance exists, the public health, safety or welfare immediately requires the closing of the property and the court then shall direct that any actions necessary to physically close down the property take place. If the property is closed down, the owner may be required to provide reasonable moving assistance to any tenant who is ordered to vacate the premises if the court finds that the tenant was not involved in the nuisance.

The law also has essentially the same provisions for commercial property that is found to be engaging in the same or similar conduct.

Keep in mind that there is also a federal law which allows the federal government to seize and sell property that has engaged in criminal drug activity.

The above law will come into effect sometime in July and will require a much more aggressive action on the part of the owners when alleged criminal activity is brought to their attention.

Finally, under the new "Slumlord" Act, it is mandatory for the owner of rental property to maintain with the Assessor, in the county where the property is located, information about the owner. The owner is required to update any information required by the Assessor's Office. That information will include the name, address and telephone number of the property owner. If the property is owned by a corporation, limited liability company, partnership, trust or real estate investment, the name, address and telephone number of the statutory agent and, if applicable, the name of a corporate officer, general partner, managing or administrative member or trustee. Also, the street address and parcel number of the property must be provided and the year the building was built. If an owner of rental property lives outside the state, he must designate and record with the Assessor a statutory agent who lives in the state and will accept legal service on his behalf. The statutory agent must provide his name, address and telephone number. No rental property can be occupied if this information is not on file with the County Assessor. This information is public record and a person who fails to comply shall be assessed a civil penalty of $1,000.00 plus an additional $100.00 per month for each month after the date of the original violation until compliance occurs.

SAMPLE FORMS

Rental Agreement 97-102

Access 103

Notice of Abandonment 104

Notice of Location of Abandoned Personal Property 105

Notice of Intent to Terminate Rental Agreement for Non-payment of Rent (Five Day Notice) 106

Partial Payment Waiver Agreement and Promissory Note (Termination for Non-payment) ... 107

Notice of Intention to Terminate for Material Breach of Rental Agreement 108

10-day Notice of Intention to Terminate Rental Agreement for Second Non-compliance Violation 109

Immediate Termination Notice 110

Thirty Day Termination Notice 111

Rental Agreement

_____, as Manager and Agent (Hereinafter "Management" for owner, rents to Resident(s),jointly and severally, the premises located at _____ unit #_____ _____, Arizona to be used solely for the purpose of a personal residence by (Name each Occupant):

(1) _____Social Security Number _____

(2) _____Social Security Number _____

(3) _____Social Security Number _____

(4) _____Social Security Number _____

for a term of _____ month(s) beginning _____, and ending _____, _____
for a furnished ☐ unfurnished ☐ apartment, and Resident(s) shall pay rent, tax, charges and deposits as set forth below. Occupancy is limited to those persons named above only.

MONTHLY RENTAL CHARGES

Rent _____
Pet Rent _____
Parking Rent _____
Other _____

_____

Subtotal _____
City Sales Tax _____
(Applicable rate subject to change during lease term)

TOTAL MONTHLY RENT $_____

OTHER CHARGES AND DEPOSITS

Security Deposit _____
Pet Deposit _____

Non-Refundable
Preparation Charge _____

Non-Refundable
Pet Sanitizing Charge _____

UTILITIES:
Natural Gas Paid By: Owner
Electric Paid By: Resident

OTHER TERMS AND CONDITIONS: _____
_____

SAMPLE

RENT PAYMENT. The rent shall be $_____ per month plus applicable sales tax payable in advance on or before the 1st day of each month at the location designated by Management, which is payable with a personal check, cashier's check, certified check or money order in the exact amount due. No second party checks will be accepted. Resident will pay as additional rent no later than the next rental payment date: (1) $_____ per day for each day after the _____ that any portion of the rent is delinquent; (2) $_____ for each non-sufficient fund check returned by the Resident's bank and thereafter all future rent and charges shall be paid only in the form of cashier's check or money order. (3) The costs or repairs caused by damages due to act of neglect by Resident's guest, and (4) $_____ fine for bringing an unauthorized pet on the property. Resident's failure to pay any rent or any other charges due many provide basis for termination of the Rental Agreement at the option of Management. Resident further agrees that Management has the exclusive right to determine how Resident's payments are applied towards the various monetary obligations of this Rental Agreement (i.e. rent, unpaid deposits, charges and/or pet permit violations).

UTILITY COST ADJUSTMENT DURING LEASE TERM. Management shall have the right, upon thirty (30) days notice to Resident, to increase the total rent due by an amount reasonably related to any increase in the cost of utilities, for either electricity and/or natural gas, if applicable.

PARKING POLICIES. Resident agrees that only those vehicles (including trailers and boats) identified below may park on the property without separate written consent from Management.

MAKE/MODEL	TYPE	YEAR	LICENSE NO.	STATE	SPACE NO.

Management may assign parking spaces or areas for residents and guests. Management may also designate: (1) No Parking areas; (2) Whether trailers, boats, or campers may park and where inoperable, abandoned or unauthorized vehicles will be towed away at the owner's expense after a _____ hour notice is posted on vehicle. The 24-hour notice does not apply to vehicles that are parked in a space assigned to another resident, parked in a marked tow-away zone or parked to impede traffic or trash collection easements. Vehicles parked in this manner will e towed away immediately without warning at owner's expense. If Management pays resident's towing expenses, such expense shall be deemed as additional rent owed and be immediately due and payable. Guests must only use unassigned spaces. Vehicle repairs may only be done with Management's permission and in areas and at times specified by Management. Motorcycles must be parked in parking lots, never on sidewalks, in landscape areas or apartments and must not damage asphalt, etc. Vehicles parked on the property must park "head in" only and show current registration. Management may elect to charge as additional rent a $_____ fine for repeat offenders.

ACCESS. Management will not enter Resident's unit without prior notice except to deal with an emergency. Resident further agrees that this notification to Management of service or maintenance request grants Management authority to enter the unit at all reasonable times for the purpose of that request, and Management must have advance written permission from Resident to open Resident's unit for others (i.e. delivery personnel, service personnel, friends, etc.). Resident is aware that under these circumstances Management is not responsible for lost or stolen articles, damage or doors left unlocked.

RESIDENT'S POLICIES. (A) Resident shall not decorate or alter the unit, patio or balcony area, change door locks, add a new lock, have a waterbed, sublet or park a motorized vehicle in the apartment, without written permission from Management. (B) Resident further agrees to comply with state statutes and city ordinances, which are applicable to the premises. (C) Resident shall show due consideration for his neighbors and not interfere with other residents' quiet enjoyment, and Management shall be sole judge of acceptable conduct. (D) Resident has carefully inspected the premises and finds them to be in a clean, rentable, undamaged condition except as may be noted otherwise in the unit inventory. Resident agrees to exercise reasonable care in the use of the premises and maintain and redeliver the same in a clean, safe and undamaged condition. (E) Guest(s) of the Resident are limited to _____ per apartment and must have Management's written consent if they stay in the apartment more than _____ days.

ABANDONMENT. Abandonment means absence of the Resident from the dwelling unit, without notice to Management for at least seven (7) days, if rent for the unit is outstanding and unpaid for ten (10) days and there is no reasonable evidence, other than the presence of the Resident's personal property, that the Resident is occupying the unit. Such abandonment shall not constitute a "surrender" without the consent of Management and in the event of abandonment, Management shall be entitled to all remedies at law or in equity, which provides that if personal property is abandoned by the Resident and determined by Management to be of less value than the cost of moving, storage and conducting a sale of such personal property, Management may destroy or otherwise dispose of any or all of the abandoned property.

COMMUNITY POLICIES. The community policies, if applicable, are for the mutual benefit of all residents and are deemed a part hereof of this Rental Agreement and violations or breaches of any community policy shall constitute a default under the Rental Agreement.

DISCLOSURE. _____ is the Owner under this Lease and service of process can be made through its statutory agent. All other notices must be in writing and delivered to the Manager's Office during regular business hours or sent by registered or certified mail to the Manager's Office during regular business hours, except as may be provided by Addendum to this Lease.

OPTION TO RENEW/RENT INCREASE. At expiration of this Lease, this Lease will automatically renew on a month-to-month basis under the same terms and conditions unless Resident gives Management a 30-day prior written notice of Resident's intent to vacate by delivering to Management a vacate notice, or unless Management, at its sole option, chooses to so renew this Lease, and in such case, Resident agrees to vacate on the expiration date of the

Lease. The rent may increase upon the expiration date if a 30-day prior written notice of such an increase is provided to Resident. A specific length lease of greater than one month, but no longer than one year, may be required for continued occupancy.

INDEMNIFICATION. Management shall not be liable for any damage or injury to the Resident(s) or any other person, or to any property, occurring on the premises, or any part thereof, or in the common areas thereof, unless such damages is the proximate result of gross negligence or unlawful act of Management, its agency, or employees and Resident agrees to hold Management harmless from any and all claims for damages no matter how caused, except for injury or damages for which Management is legally responsible. Resident shall be responsible for obtaining fire, extended coverage and liability insurance with respect to the contents of the apartment. Resident understands that Management's insurance does not cover Resident's belongings from losses not caused by Management's negligence and Management encourages Resident to obtain an all-risk policy in addition to marking all valuables for "Operation Identification".

WAIVER. Failure of Management to insist upon strict compliance with the terms of this Rental Agreement shall not constitute a waiver of Management's rights to act on any violation.

ATTORNEY'S FEES. In the event of legal action to enforce compliance with this Rental Agreement, the prevailing party may be awarded court costs and reasonable attorney's fees.

SEVERABILITY. If any provision of this Rental Agreement is invalid under applicable law, such provisions shall be ineffective to the extent of such invalidity only, without invalidating the remainder of this Rental Agreement.

REMEDIES CUMULATIVE. All remedies under this Rental Agreement of by law or equity shall be cumulative.

SECURITY. Resident hereby agrees and acknowledges that Management and Owner shall not provide and shall have no duty to provide any security services to Resident or the community. Resident shall look solely to the public police force for security protection and Resident agrees and acknowledges that protection against criminal action is not within the power of Management and Owner, and, even if from time to time Management provides security services, those services cannot be relied upon by Resident and shall not constitute a waiver of, or in any manner modify the above agreement. Management and Owner shall not be liable for failure to provide adequate security services or for criminal or wrongful actions by others against Resident, Resident's relatives or Resident's guests.

TRANSFERS. Military personnel on active duty may terminate the Rental Agreement upon receipt of orders transferring to another base, releasing from active duty, or ordering occupancy of government quarters. Resident agrees to give as much written notice as possible and rent will be prorated from the notice date to move-out date. Assignment instructions for the voluntary occupancy of government quarters are not sufficient for termination of the Apartment Rental Agreement.

MOVE-OUT CHARGES. Resident agrees that move-out charges will be determined as follows:

♦ A. **RENT**. Resident must deliver a signed vacate Notice at least thirty (30) days prior to move-out and fulfill the agreed upon terms of the Rental Agreement. Month-to-Month Rental Agreements. Resident agrees to pay rent until the apartment is reoccupied or thirty days from the periodic rental due date or date Resident delivers his notice. Rental Agreements with more than thirty (30) days remaining. Resident agrees to pay rent until the apartment is reoccupied or until the expiration of the Rental Agreement, whichever comes first.

♦ B. **INADEQUATE CLEANING**. If Resident does not complete the cleaning requirements listed as determined by Management.

♦ C. **ADMINISTRATIVE CHARGES**. I agree to pay $_____ to defray Management's administrative and marketing costs if Resident does either of the following:
   1. Fails to fulfill the agreed upon term of the Apartment Rental Agreement, or
   2. Fails to deliver a written "VACATE NOTICE" to Management at least thirty (30) days prior to move-out.

♦ D. **PROPERTY DAMAGE**. Resident agrees that if apartment is not returned in the same condition as Resident received it, less fair wear and tear as determined by Management, Resident will be charged Management's cost to repair. Personal property remaining after move-out will be disposed of without accountability.

♦ E. **OTHER**. Resident agrees to pay any unpaid preparation fee, pet sanitizing fee, late charges, lost key charges or other unpaid charges at time of move-out. Failure to vacate on move-out date will cost me daily rent plus two month's rent or twice the Management's damages, whichever is greater as provided by law.

IMPORTANT: Management will first apply security and pet deposits to satisfy the charges listed above in Paragraphs A through E. HOWEVER, IF THESE DEPOSITS ARE INSUFFICIENT TO SATISFY THE TOTAL CHARGES, MANAGEMENT WILL SEND RESIDENT, AT THE MOST CURRENT ADDRESS RESIDENT GIVES MANAGEMENT, AN ITEMIZED BILL WHICH RESIDENT AGREES TO PAY PROMPTLY. MANAGEMENT AGREES TO RETURN ALL REFUNDABLE DEPOSITS IN ACCORDANCE WITH A.R.S. § 33-1321.

GENERAL PROVISIONS. No oral promises, representation or agreements have been made by Owner or Management. This Lease is the entire agreement between the parties and Management (including its employees, leasing personnel and other personnel) has no authority to waive, amend or terminate this Lease or any part of it and no authority to make promises, representations or agreements which impose duties of security or other obligations on Owner or Management unless done in writing. Further, Resident may obtain a copy of the Arizona Residential Landlord and Tenant Act at the Arizona Secretary of State's Office. Resident may be present at a move-out inspection of the rental unit with written notice to the Landlord. Resident further acknowledges that he/she was provided a copy of the Federal Lead Hazard pamphlet and accepts responsibility for reading and understanding its contents.

FAIR HOUSING ACCOMMODATIONS. This community is dedicated to honoring Federal and Arizona Fair Housing laws. Accommodations will be made/allowed as reasonably necessary to the policies and regulations of the community in order to enable Residents with disabilities to utilize the rental premises. The community reserves the right to require reasonable medical evidence of the disability and that the requested accommodation is necessary. The Resident may be required to restore the premises to their prior condition if failure to make restoration would interfere with the owner's or next tenant's use and enjoyment of the premises.

ADDENDUM TO APARTMENT RENTAL AGREEMENT

For the first _____ month(s) of this Agreement, Management agrees to reduce the basic monthly rent by $_____ per month with the understanding that in the event the Resident does not fully perform under the terms and conditions of this Lease. Resident agrees to return to Management any rent incentives herein accepted by Resident or reimburse Management for the full market value of said incentives.

AGREEMENT AND ACCEPTANCE. Resident agrees to (1) live within the spirit and letter of this entire agreement including the Rental Application, the Apartment, inventory and Pet Agreement (if applicable), all of which are attached; (2) that each obligation of this Agreement is material and a violation of any obligation entitles Management to terminate this Agreement and/or exercise any other legal rights it may possess; (3) that the Resident designated below as "Agent" shall deliver the total rent due each month to Management, occupy the assigned parking space (if applicable) and receive any security refund (if applicable); (4) and upon written notice from Management, this Agreement will convert to a month-to-month tenancy if false and/or misleading information is contained in the Rental Application.

Resident: **Management (Authorized Agent for the OWNER)**

_____   _____
Resident/Agent

_____   _____
                                                    (Title)

Resident date: _____   Management date: _____

ACCESS

TO: _____
    & ANY/ALL OCCUPANTS

_____

_____

PURSUANT TO A.R.S. SEC. 33-1343, your rental unit will be entered and inspected on the following date: _____ between the hours of 9:00 A.M. and 5:00 P.M., or as specified below.

Should this create an inconvenience, please contact management immediately. Failure to allow access will result in the termination of your lease and an action for possession to be immediately commenced, pursuant to A.R>S> Sec. 33-1376, without further notice to you.

DATED: _____

BY: _____

( ) **Hand Delivered this** _____ **day of** _____ **, 20** ____

( ) **Certified Mailed this** _____ **day of** _____ **, 20** ____

NOTICE OF ABANDONMENT

NOTICE IS HEREBY GIVEN that _____ is
                                      (address)
hereby abandoned as of _____. We are taking
                             (date)
this action for the following reasons:

1. There has been a lack of activity in and about these premise indicating that you have abandoned the premises.

2. You have five days from the date of this notice in which to notify the manager/owner/agent that you have, in fact, not abandoned the premises.

3. If not notified within five days from the date of this notice, the manager/owner/agent will take any action necessary to retake the premises including changing door locks, taking an inventory of any personal belongings left in the unit and placing them in storage for ten (10) days at which time they will be disposed of or sold.

4. Please call _____ for the information to regain entry to the premises and possession of the property.

DATED: _____

BY: _____

NOTICE OF LOCATION OF ABANDONED PERSONAL PROPERTY

TO: _____

RE: _____

The above referenced dwelling unit was previously deemed to have been abandoned, consistent with the provisions of A.R.S. Sec 33-1370. Thereafter, a Notice of Abandonment was duly mailed to you at your last known address by certified mail, return receipt requested. In addition, the Notice of Abandonment was posted for at least five (5) days on the door of the dwelling unit or at another conspicuous place on the property. Following this five (5) day period, the undersigned landlord took possession of the dwelling unit as allowed by law.

This notice is to inform you that any personal belongings found in the unit at this time has been removed and placed in storage. The items are located at the following location: _____
_____
_____

The subject dwelling unit and the personal property abandoned within the unit were taken into possession by the landlord on this date: _____.
The items of personal property taken at such time will be held for a period of ten (10) days beginning with the first rental date occurring after the Landlord's declaration of abandonment. If you desire to claim the personal property, you must contact the landlord promptly. After expiration of the holding time prescribed by law, such personal property will be sold or otherwise disposed of by the Landlord according to the provisions of law.

You are informed that if you notify the Landlord in writing, on or before the date the landlord sells or otherwise disposes of the personal property, that you intend to remove the personal property from the dwelling unit or place of storage, you will have five (5) days to reclaim the personal property. To reclaim the personal property, you may be required to pay the landlord for the costs of removal and storage for the period of time your personal property remained in the landlord's safekeeping.

You are further informed that the Landlord will proceed in dealing with the subject personal property according to provisions of law, particularly A.R.S. 33-1370. You may wish to review the Statute and consult an attorney to determine any rights you may have that would be affected in these regards.

Date: _____

By: _____

NOTICE OF INTENT TO TERMINATE RENTAL AGREEMENT FOR NON-PAYMENT OF RENT (FIVE DAY NOTICE)

To: _____
& ANY/ALL OCCUPANTS

_____   UNIT NO. _____

_____

Please be advised that the filing of a lawsuit against you for Forcible Detainer by
_____ (owner/management) is imminent
because you have been in arrears on the payment of your rent for the above named premises
since _____, in the amount of $ _____. As provided in your
rental agreement, this sum includes late charges of $ _____ per _____, which will
continue to accrue at that rate.

If legal action is instituted, not only is it likely that the Court will award Judgment to the
Owner/Management Company for the above sum and order that you vacate the premises, but it is likely
that you will be ordered to pay all court costs and attorney fees.

We would like to give you an opportunity to resolve this matter prior to the initiation of legal action. It will
save all involved time, energy and money. To do so, you must contact your property manager immediately
and deliver the full sum due.

Absent the above action, be advised that, pursuant to Arizona Revised Statutes Sec. 12-1171(a)(1), it is
hereby demanded that you surrender the above described premises forthwith. If you have not complied
with the demand for possession on the fifth (5) day after notice herein, you will be deemed by law to be in
forcible detainer.

Further, pursuant to A.R.S. Sec. 33-1368(B), you are hereby notified that each day your rent continues to
be delinquent, within a minimum of five (5) days from the date hereof, will, without further act or notice by
management, result in the immediate termination of your rental agreement as of this date:
_____ or five (5) days after receipt of this notice. Management expressly does not waive
the right to bring an action against you for all unpaid rent from the date of your vacating the premises until
such time as the property is re-rented or your fixed term lease expires, whichever comes first. You are
given notice herein that you shall be liable for said sums.

If you fail to pay the aforesaid sum, plus any additional late charges within the time specified herein and
continue to occupy the premises past the termination date, legal action will be brought against you for
eviction and recovery of possession, monetary damages, reasonable attorney fees and court costs.
Furthermore, if your occupancy beyond the termination date is intentional, then pursuant to A.R.S. Sec.
33-1375, as amended, you may also be subject to additional damages equal to twice your monthly rent or
twice management's actual damages, whichever is greater. Please be further advised that your deposit
may not be used for rent. Pursuant to A.R.S. 33-1321, the deposit or an itemization of damages will be
sent to you at your forwarding address within fourteen (14) business days of your vacating the premises
and return of all keys. The premises must be left in a clean and undamaged condition.

You are liable for the full term of your lease and will be held to the full term of your lease or until the
premises are re-rented. If you are on a month to month tenancy, then you are liable for al unpaid rent from
the date you vacate the property and an additional thirty day period or the re-rent date, whichever comes
first.

( ) Hand Delivered this date: _____

( ) Certified Mailed this date: _____

By:_____

PARTIAL PAYMENT WAIVER AGREEMENT
AND PROMISSORY NOTE
(TERMINATION FOR NON-PAYMENT)

In consideration of my occupancy after _____, I promise to
pay _____ my unpaid rent in the amount of _____
, which includes properly assessed late charges of _____, payable as follows:

        DATE DUE   AMOUNT   PAID THRU DATE

In accordance with A.R.S. Sec. 33-1371, I understand and agree that Management does not
waive its right under law or under my Rental Agreement. I re-affirm my agreement to pay rent
not later than the First day of each month. I also understand and agree that I am currently in
default on the payment of my rent.

Pursuant to Article 5, Chapter 10, 33-1368(B), as amended, I am hereby notified that my failure
to pay the above amount plus the _____ per day for each additional day my rent is
delinquent, within five (5) days from the date hereof my rent is not paid in full or if I do not make
all payments according to the schedule above without further act or notice by Management will
result in termination of my rental agreement.

I further agree and understand if I default on any payments due under this agreement, a Writ of
Restitution can be filed without further notice. Furthermore, if my occupancy beyond the
termination date is intentional, then pursuant to A.R.S. Sec. 33-1375, as amended, I may also be
subject to additional damages to twice my monthly rent or twice Management's actual damages,
whichever is greater.

I further agree that, _____ (Owner/Agent), by entering into this
agreement, is not waiving its legal remedies against me for the possession of the premises,
including commoning a Forcible Detainer action to regain possession of the premises and
obtain a Judgment for accrued and unpaid rent, or if Judgment has been entered, re-taking
possession of the premises, pursuant to a Writ of Restitution if necessary, should I default the
terms and conditions herein. I further waive any and all rights I may have under A.R.S.Sec. 33-
1371.

        Dated this _____ day of _____ , 20 _____

_____   _____
TENANT   LANDLORD

NOTICE OF INTENTION TO TERMINATE FOR MATERIAL BREACH OF RENTAL AGREEMENT

TO: _____   DATE: _____

    & ANY/ALL OCCUPANTS

_____

_____

Please be advised the pursuant to Arizona Revised Statutes, Sec. 33-1368(a), your rental agreement, dated _____ for the above described premises, shall terminate ten (10) days (five days for health & safety) from the date of your receipt, as defined by law, of this notice if you have not completely and permanently remedied the following defaults within the above time limits.

Explanation of violations:

Your failure to comply in full with this notice will result in the termination of your right of possession, under your rental agreement within ten (10) days (five days for health & safety) from the date of your receipt, as defined by law, of this notice and the immediate filing of a special detainer action in which you additionally may be liable for accrued rent, late charges and attorney fees, and costs and/or such other remedial action to which the owner or its representative may be entitled to by law. This notice and any action taken pursuant to it by the owner or its representative may not be construed as, and is not intended as, waiver of other rights or remedies or an election of remedies.

In the event you commit or permit the reoccurance of defaults which are the same or similar to those defaults specified above during the term of your lease, your rental agreement will terminate within ten (10) days after delivery by owner or its representative of a written notice advising you of your second noncompliance, and owner and/or its representatives will be entitled to file a special detainer action and/or pursue any other remedies available under the law.

By: _____

( ) **Hand Delivered this** _____ day of _____ , 20 ____

( ) **Certified Mailed this** _____ day of _____ , 20 ____

10 DAY NOTICE OF INTENT TO TERMINATE RENTAL AGREEMENT FOR SECOND NON COMPLIANCE VIOLATION

DATE: _____

TO: _____
     & ANY/ALL OCCUPANTS

_____

_____

Please be advised that pursuant to Arizona Revised Statutes Sec. 33-1368A, your rental agreement dated _____ for the above described premises shall terminate TEN (10) days from the date of your receipt (as defined by law) of this notice for the reason that there has been a second non-compliance of the same or similar nature involving the previous notice to you dated _____.

The violation(s) is:

Your failure to comply in full with this notice will result in the filing of a Forcible Detainer Action against you to remove you from the premises. The Landlord may be entitled to all rent due and owing, plus attorney fees and costs. Furthermore, pursuant to A. R. S. 33-1375C, if your hold-over is considered intentional and not in good faith, the Landlord will request all appropriate damages pursuant to said statute.

By: _____

( ) **Hand Delivered this** _____ **day of** _____ , **20** ____

( ) **Certified Mailed this** _____ **day of** _____ , **20** ____

IMMEDIATE TERMINATION NOTICE

TO: _____   DATE: _____

     & ANY/ALL OCCUPANTS

_____

_____

IT HAS COME TO MANAGEMENT'S ATTENTION that you, members of your family or your guests have engaged in material and irreparable conduct in and about the premises, including the following:

Because of such conduct, please be advised that you have irreparably breached material provisions of your rental agreement and that Management has, pursuant to A.R.S. 33-1368(A), terminated such agreement effective herewith. Demand is hereby made that you vacate your apartment immediately. Should you fail to do so, an action will be commenced against you in Forcible Detainer for recovery of possession and damages.

Moreover, should your hold-over of the premises beyond such date and time be willful and not in good faith, then pursuant to A.R.S. Sec. 33-1362(C) and 33-1375(C), you will be liable for twice your monthly rental rate, or twice the actual damages to Management, whichever is greater. Should any of these remedies be commenced against you, you will also be liable for court costs and attorney fees.

Should you wish to avoid the costs and remedies set forth herein above, you are advised to vacate the premises immediately.

BY:_____

( ) **Hand Delivered this** _____ day of _____ , 20 _____

( ) **Certified Mailed this** _____ day of _____ , 20 _____

THIRTY DAY TERMINATION NOTICE

To: _____
      & Any/All Occupants

_____

_____

PURSUANT TO ARIZONA REVISED STATUTES SEC. 33-1375B, your rental agreement with _____ for the premises above will terminate thirty (30) days from the date of this notice. Your next periodic rental due date you must vacate by the following date: _____.

Please remove yourself from the premises on or before that date and pay any outstanding rent due at that time to management. If you fail to vacate, your holdover may be considered wilfull and entitle your landlord to two months rentor actual damages, whichever is greater, **PURSUANT TO A.R.S. SEC. 33-1375(C).** All rent should be paid as per your rental agreement. You may not use your security or other deposits towards the rent payment.

DATE: _____

BY: _____

( ) **Hand Delivered this** _____ **day of** _____ , 20 _____

( ) **Certified Mailed this** _____ **day of** _____ , 20 _____

Informational Agencies

Chambers of Commerce

Apache Junction
112 East 2nd Avenue
Apache Junction, Arizona 85219
Phone: (480) 982-3141

Arizona
1221 East Osborn, No. 100
Phoenix, Arizona 85014
Phone: (602) 248-9172

Avondale-Goodyear-Litchfield Park
501 West Van Buren, No. K
Avondale, Arizona 85323
Phone: (623) 932-2260

Carefree/Cave Creek
6710 E. Cave Creek Rd.
Cave Creek, Arizona 85331
Phone: (480) 488-3381

Chandler
218 North Arizona Avenue
Chandler, Arizona 85225
Phone: (480) 963-4571

Flagstaff
101 West Santa Fe Avenue, W. Rt. 66
Flagstaff, Arizona 86001-5598
Phone: (520) 774-4505

Fountain Hills
16837 Palisades/P. O. Box 17598
Fountain Hills, Arizona 85269
Phone: (480) 837-1654

Gilbert
202 North Gilbert Road
Gilbert, Arizona 85234
Phone: (480) 892-0056

Glendale
7105 North 59th Avenue
Glendale, Arizona 85301
Phone: (623) 937-4754

Greater Paradise Valley
2737 East Greenway Road, No. 10
Phoenix, Arizona 85032-4319
Phone: (602) 482-3344

Mesa
120 North Center
Mesa, Arizona 85201
Phone: (480) 969-1307

Peoria
8355 West Peoria
Peoria, Arizona 85345
Phone: (623) 979-3601

Phoenix Metropolitan
201 North Central, 27th Floor
Phoenix, Arizona 85073
Phone: (602) 254-5521

Scottsdale
7343 Scottsdale Mall
Scottsdale, Arizona 85251
Phone: (480) 945-8481

Tempe
909 East Apache Blvd.
Tempe, Arizona 85285
Phone: (480) 967-7891

Tucson
P.O. Box 991
Tucson, Arizona 85701
Phone: (520) 792-1212

Convention and Visitors Bureaus

Metropolitan Tucson
130 South Scott Avenue
Tucson, Arizona 85701
Phone: (520) 624-1817

Phoenix & Valley of the Sun
400 East Van Buren, Suite 600
Phoenix, Arizona 85004
Phone: (602) 254-6500

Others

Mexican Chamber of Commerce
4644 North 38th Drive
Phoenix, Arizona 85019
Phone: (602) 252-6448

Arizona Multi-Housing Association
2400 E. Az. Biltmore Circle, Ste. 1200
Phoenix, Arizona 85016
Phone: (602) 224-0135

Community Legal Services .... **(602) 258-3434**